A
GREAT PLACE
TO
Grow Old

PRAISE FOR *A GREAT PLACE TO GROW OLD*:

'We live in a society, and sometimes a church, that doesn't always appreciate the gifts that older people bring. Tina English brings a great deal of wisdom, huge experience, practical advice and ideas together in this invaluable guide to a vital and growing ministry in local churches. If you want to know where to start with ministry among older people, this is a great place to begin.'

THE RT REVD DR GRAHAM TOMLIN, BISHOP OF KENSINGTON

'The time is so ripe for this book. It's super-accessible and I can hear Tina speaking as she guides us through practical, imaginative, ways to support and learn from older people. She's longing to see everyone enjoy life in all its fullness.'

DEBBIE THROWER,
PIONEER, ANNA CHAPLAINCY FOR OLDER PEOPLE

'This timely, informed and succinct resource will equip churches and communities to identify and address the needs of older people in a post-COVID world.'

ALBERT JEWELL, SECRETARY OF CHRISTIANS ON AGEING
DEMENTIA NETWORK, FORMER PASTORAL DIRECTOR AND SENIOR
CHAPLAIN OF MHA CARE GROUP

'With society all too often marginalising older people, this book reflects on what God has to say about old people and challenges us on how that should impact our behaviours and attitude. Written with a refreshing honesty and authenticity, it poses insightful questions as well as providing reams of information to equip us to go and reach older people with the love of Jesus.'

CARL KNIGHTLY, CEO OF FAITH IN LATER LIFE, SPEAKER
AND MEDIA COMMENTATOR

'I was introduced to Tina English through one of the couples referred to in this book. The glowing reports I heard made me hope that one day Tina would share her wisdom and insights more widely. In this book she most certainly has. Almost daily I hear a mixture of stories, some from young and vibrant congregations and some from elderly ones, and the younger ones want to know how to reach out to the elderly and the elderly ones want to know how to reach the young. Armed with the information in the book, no one need be left redundant. There is a whole world of care that we can all be engaged in, regardless of our age. An important section of our communities deserves the best.'

REV DR HUGH OSGOOD, PRESIDENT OF CHURCHES IN
COMMUNITIES INTERNATIONAL AND FREE CHURCHES
PRESIDENT OF CHURCHES TOGETHER IN ENGLAND

A
GREAT PLACE
TO
Grow Old

RE-IMAGINING MINISTRY AMONG
OLDER PEOPLE

TINA ENGLISH

DARTON · LONGMAN + TODD

First published in 2021 by
Darton, Longman and Todd Ltd
1 Spencer Court
140 – 142 Wandsworth High Street
London SW18 4JJ

ISBN: 978-0-232-53458-0

A catalogue record for this book is available from the British Library.

Cover photograph by Ivan Kmit/Dreamstime.com

Designed and produced by Judy Linard

Printed and bound in Great Britain by Bell & Bain, Glasgow

THIS BOOK IS DEDICATED TO MY
WONDERFUL MUM AND DAD,
BARBARA AND ALAN SARGENT,
WHO POUR OUT THEIR LIVES FOR THE
BLESSING OF OTHERS.

CONTENTS

PREFACE

I was invited to run a seminar at a Christian conference on how the church should be a place of radical hospitality for older people. The organiser asked for book recommendations they could stock up on for the conference, but to my dismay, I realised that despite a shelf full of books, there wasn't one that I could wholeheartedly recommend.

Don't get me wrong, there are some good books already in print if you're interested in the spirituality or theology of ageing, or if you're after some tips on how to grow old gracefully. That's not what this book is about. I wanted a book that took a fresh look at ministry amongst older people, that was theologically based but practical. A book that was easy to read, full of inspiring ideas and gave real examples from experienced practitioners. A book that recognised that older age today looks different from how it did 20 years ago.

If you are someone who is also looking for a book like that, I hope this offering hits the spot. If you are a church leader who recognises that our population is ageing and you want to know how you can respond, then read on. If you are a Christian involved in ministry amongst seniors, I hope this book will be an encouragement that cheers you on in the valuable work that you are doing. If you are someone with a heart for older people and seeking to find expression for it, this book is brimming with tried and tested ideas.

I've started with some underlying principles and theology that seek to communicate God's heart for older people, and then we dive into the practical, looking at how we can come alongside those living with dementia, carers and care home residents. We'll go on to explore ideas for ministry amongst seniors if you have an accessible church building. But what if you don't? There are many newer churches these days that don't have their own premises – does that mean you can't come alongside your older community in meaningful, effective ways? Of course not, and we'll look at lots of ideas for reaching out beyond the four walls of a building.

We'll then take some time to consider what our mission and vision is for ministry amongst older people. With so many ideas and suggestions you might be left wondering what to do and where to start, so we'll focus on that in the final chapter, along with some other general principles and practicalities.

This book has been revised in light of the COVID-19 pandemic, which brought the widespread issues of loneliness and isolation to the fore, and accelerated the use of video-calling technology to promote togetherness. The post-pandemic world is an ideal time to review the ministry and mission of your church in reaching out and discipling older people.

I have included stories of actual projects and people throughout this book. Where I have permission I have used real names, but where individuals do not have capacity to give consent I have changed the names and some of the factual details so that they remain anonymous.

Acknowledgements

This book would not have been possible without the contributions of many people who are doing amazing work amongst the over-65s. Thank you to everyone who has shared their experience, including Buddy Reeve, Chris Dodgson, Coryn Robinson, David Jolley, Debbie Thrower, Gemma Gillard, Ian Jones, Jane Stephens, Jeanette Main, Jeremy Sharpe, Louise Maclay, Peter Meadows, Pippa Cramer, Sarah Williams and Victoria Byrne. I have so appreciated the input from the Carers Connected group who have given me valuable insights into the experience of family carers. I am particularly grateful to Sandra Kimber and Liz Stacey who not only shared their experience with me, but patiently listened and gave advice when I needed to clarify my thoughts.

A special thank you to John Noble and Jeannette Harrison who opened up about their journeys of caring for a loved one with dementia, and have encouraged me in putting pen to paper. And thank you to Ron, Michael, Mary and Joy for allowing me to share your stories.

I used to think I was good at grammar until I asked people to proof read this book. I am indebted to Jeanette Main, Judy Franklin, Liz Windaybank, Ciara Pearman and Victoria Byrne for correcting my grammatical errors and typos.

Finally, thank you to my wonderful family for your support and patience, while I've spent hours at a computer.

CHAPTER 1

A GREAT PLACE TO GROW OLD

Beryl sat alone in her room looking longingly at the beautiful park across the road. Majestic trees and wild scrubland delighted her with a scenic view that transformed with the seasons, but as she watched people strolling along, she couldn't help but yearn to go there herself. Beryl was a frail, unassuming lady in her 80s with Parkinson's disease and dementia, who loved nature, and had moved to the care home to be close to her son. She had bought a wheelchair in the hope that he would take her across to the park, but for whatever reason, this hadn't happened. So Beryl spent most of her days sitting alone in her room, overlooked and ignored by most of society.

The danger of starting with a true story like this, is that it can reinforce stereotypes. Not all older people are lonely or needy, and the majority do not live in care homes. But the Church is called to make disciples, and discipleship is a lifelong process, with new challenges presented to us at each stage of life, from childhood to our years of grey hair and wrinkles. How do we journey with people through these latter years in a way that encourages them to live and experience later life in all its fullness? How do we help Beryl to experience the reality of God's love for her? These questions are important to answer because our population is ageing and the Church is ageing faster than the rest of society. To give you an idea of the rate of change, between 2012 and 2017 the number of people living to be 100 increased by 85 per cent.[1] By 2030 it's predicted that 1 in 5 people will be over 65,[2] and the over 85 age group is the fastest growing, forecast to double in the next 20 years.[3]

It would be a mistake to view these changes negatively, as there is much to celebrate: we are living longer due to health improvements, with many childhood illnesses eradicated through immunisations, and new treatments available for diseases such as diabetes, heart disease and cancer. And we need to bust the myth that older people are somehow a drain on the nation's resources. Not only is this a negative, derogatory mindset towards older people, it's a distortion of reality. Most retired folk have spent a large part of their lives working, contributing to the public purse through taxation, as well as contributing to society in other ways as neighbours and informal carers, not to mention the war effort. These contributions do not stop in older age. Research shows the highest level of volunteering amongst older people, compared to other age groups[4] and the informal care provided by older people is huge: nearly 54 million hours in the UK, worth an estimated £11.4bn.[5]

THE CHURCH AND AN AGEING POPULATION

The Church is ageing faster than society as a whole due to the drop in numbers of young people attending.[6] In 2000, the over 65s accounted for 25 per cent of congregation members, and this has steadily grown so that by 2030 it is predicted that 45 per cent of churchgoers will be over 65. Similar to society as a whole, the over 85 age group is the fastest growing, accounting for just 5 per cent of the over 65s congregation at the start of the millennium, and predicted to rise to 19 per cent by 2030.

How should the Church respond to an ageing congregation? It's not enough to plough resources into encouraging young people back into the church. As important as this is, we are still living in a society that is ageing, and our desire should be discipleship across every age group. The Bible tells us that the church should be a good place to grow old in. Zechariah 8:4–5 declares:

> Old men and old women will come back to Jerusalem, sit on benches on the streets and spin tales, move around safely with their canes – a good city to grow old in. And boys and girls will fill the public parks, laughing and playing – a good city to grow up in. (*The Message*)

Jerusalem is often seen to represent the Church, suggesting that the church should be a good place to grow up in and a good place to grow old in. In recent years there has been much-needed focus on church being a good place to grow up in – on youth and children's ministries – but it's also vital to consider what it means for the church to be a good place to grow old. This raises an important question – what do we mean by old?

WHAT'S IN A NUMBER?

At what age is someone officially old? 65? 85? 95? Your answer probably depends on how old you are. A four-year-old was recently asked on a television programme, 'How old is really old?' What do you think her answer was? The best definition I have heard to the question, 'How old is old?' came from a retired member of my church who said it was, 'Ten years older than me!' Most of us, as the years start clocking up, don't feel old, and we tend to view the people who are older than us as the ones who are aged. That's as true when you're 35 as it is when you're 85! The four-year-old on TV thought that 30 was really old!

I remember, as a nurse, seeing a patient who came to us at the age of 96 because her legs had become swollen and she could no longer put on her riding boots. She liked to ride her horse every day in Hyde Park and her swollen legs were proving quite inconvenient! At 96 she may have been well advanced in years, but she was more active than many folk a lot younger.

Rather than thinking numerically, it can be helpful to consider growing older in terms of the third and fourth ages of life.[7] The third age is the period post-retirement where individuals are physically and cognitively well and able to enjoy an active life. In contrast, the fourth age is where frailty increases and physical or cognitive decline reduces the capacity of an individual to live actively and independently. In this framework it's quite possible for my 96-year-old patient to be seen in the third age of life, whereas someone who is 65 but housebound might be considered in the fourth age.

All too often we group older people into one homogenous category when, in reality, the over 65s comprise a number of distinct generations. We wouldn't think to put a two-year-old into the same generation as a 22-year-old, and yet we readily put someone who is 65 in the same category as someone who is 85. The latter will have experienced the war years, which will have greatly impacted their world view, along with an appreciation of the need to 'make do and mend'. People born in the immediate post-war years, the baby boomers, may see the world differently as they grew up in a more affluent, consumer-driven society.

Although people may have a sense of identity as part of a generation, whether that's as baby boomers, Generation X, Y or Z, and may share a similar cultural experience, that's not to suggest that people of the same generation all think the same! I'm an 80s girl (a teenager in the 80s, not born then!), or Generation X, and I love the heritage of 80s music, but when I read about the supposed characteristics and cultural experiences of my generation, it does not all ring true to me: I'm uniquely different from my contemporaries, as are you.

How we view older people will determine whether the church is a good place to grow old in. There's a temptation to view older people as of less value, because we think they are not able to contribute – as if our value is based on what we do, or what we can give. We've already debunked the myth that older people don't contribute to society, but even if they are not able to give so much, when the frailty of the fourth age limits their ability to live actively and independently, does that mean they are of less value? When people start losing their cognition or their independence, are they somehow less of a person? Do they lose their worth? What is our worth and value as human beings based on?

Too often society can associate the worth and value of individuals with their productivity. I think there's a danger of this attitude slipping into the church – we do love to have people who can fill slots on our rotas! More than that, I have heard people espousing the value of older people with the fact that they have so much to give. Indeed, they do have so much to give, but that's not where their value lies! In fact, across every age group there's a danger of valuing people for what they can contribute rather than for who they are. And perhaps we can all think of times in our life when we have felt like this, people only wanting us for what we can do. It's demoralising, exhausting and soul destroying.

So, if our value doesn't lie in what we contribute, where does it lie? Fortunately, the Bible gives us an answer. Let's explore four elements of what the Bible tells us about what it means to be human, to be a person, and consider not only how our value is derived from these, but also that they never change, no matter how young or old we are. As human beings we are dependent; created in the image of God; loved and relational.[8]

WE ARE DEPENDENT

We place so much value on independence, yet God has created us to be dependent as human beings – dependent on Him and dependent on one another.

When John Stott, a famous Christian theologian, was in his 80s he fell and fractured his hip, leading to a season of ill health where he was dependent on others. Reflecting on that time, he wrote:

> We come into this world totally dependent on the love, care and protection of others. We go through a phase of life when other people are dependent on us. And most of us will go out of this world totally dependent on the love and care of others. And this is not an evil, destructive reality. It is part of the design; part of the physical nature God has given us.
>
> I sometimes hear old people, including Christian people who should know better, say 'I don't want to be a burden to anyone else. I'm happy to carry on living so long as I can look after myself but as soon as I become a burden I would rather die.' But this is wrong. We are all designed to be a burden to others. You are designed to be a burden to me and I am designed to be a burden to you. And the life of the family, including the life of the local church family, should be one of 'mutual burdensomeness'. 'Carry each other's burdens and in this way you will fulfil the law of Christ.' (Gal 6:2)

Christ himself takes on the dignity of dependence. He is born a baby, totally dependent on the care of his mother. He needs to be fed, he needs his bottom to be wiped, he needs to be propped up when he rolls over. And yet he never loses his divine dignity. And at the end, on the cross, he again becomes totally dependent, limbs pierced and stretched, unable to move. So in the person of Christ we learn that dependence does not, cannot, deprive a person of their dignity, of their supreme worth. And if dependence was appropriate for the God of the universe, it is certainly appropriate for us.[9]

We are designed for dependence! Jesus modelled this dependence with His disciples. When He sent out the Twelve, He told them to take nothing with them for the journey.[10] I had always assumed that this was so that they would be dependent on God, and this is true to some extent. But also, He is putting them in a position where they will have to be dependent on others. They were given instructions to search for a worthy person and stay in their house. Dependence on others – it's part of God's design for our lives.

CREATED IN THE IMAGE OF GOD

As human beings we are created in the image of God. In the first book of the Bible we are told: 'So God created mankind in his own image, in the image of God He created him; male and female he created them.'[11] Chapter 2 goes on to say: 'Then the LORD God formed a man from the dust of the ground and breathed into his nostrils the breath of life, and the man became a living being.'[12]

How awe-inspiring to appreciate that at the dawn of creation God breathed His life into human beings – that's how we came into existence. And we are made in His image – the only part of His creation that is specifically made in His likeness. That's why Jesus could say, 'Whenever you did one of these things to someone overlooked or ignored, that was me – you did it to me.'[13]

You've probably heard Descartes' saying, 'I think, therefore I am.' But no, our *raison d'être* isn't in our cognitive ability, or our physical ability for that matter. What if my cognitive ability is impaired and I can't think clearly anymore? Am I less of a person? No! God has breathed His life into me, therefore I am. This is an unchangeable truth – it remains true throughout our lives, whatever our circumstances. A frail person with dementia in the fourth age of life is still created in the image of God, with intrinsic value and worth endowed on them by the creator of the universe.

Our identity flows from this unique privilege to bear His image. When we submit our lives to Jesus, we become sons and daughters of the King of kings, adopted into His family. I am a daughter of the King of kings! If you have submitted your life to Jesus, then you are a son or daughter of the King. And that is an identity built on a solid foundation – it is never going to change. People in the third and fourth ages of life, who have submitted their lives to Jesus, are sons and daughters of the King. What a status, what a responsibility, what a privilege! And those who don't know Jesus yet are sons and daughters in waiting – God's desire is that they too are adopted into His family.

WE ARE LOVED

It's no surprise that God desires to adopt all men and women into His family, since as human beings we are loved – deeply, widely, far more than we could ever imagine. I am loved, you are loved, people in the third and fourth ages of life are deeply loved.

The apostle John, in his advanced years, reflecting on all the incredible things he had seen, heard and experienced, kept coming back to God's love: 'See what great love the Father has lavished on us, that we should be called children of God! And that is what we are!'[14]

If we are going to start a ministry amongst older people, if we are going to reach out with God's love, then we need to know how loved we are, so that God's unconditional love can overflow from us to others. Meditate on the truth of those words for a few minutes and let them go from your head to your heart. When we really know how loved we are, we will be empowered to change the world!

We are not loved for anything we have done, haven't done, can do or can't do. We are loved. Full stop. God doesn't love us because we love and serve Him. He initiated – He reached out in love to us while we were separated from Him. The Bible tells us, 'While we were still sinners, Christ died for us',[15] and that it was God's love for us that motivated Him to send Jesus.[16]

These are basic biblical truths but sometimes they are easy to forget when we've been Christians for a while. We slip into performance mode and it becomes about what we do: I haven't read my Bible enough, prayed enough, reached out enough, been holy enough, etc. We compare ourselves to either our own ideal, from which we fall far short, or to others who we perceive as better or worse than us. But comparison just leads to disaster. We either end up feeling discouraged, or self-righteous, if the balance of good deeds and holiness tips in our favour. Both mindsets end up distancing us from God, because it was never about our performance. Think of a baby in its mother's arms: it doesn't have to do anything – it is loved! Yes, a baby will have to grow and learn to do stuff, like walking, feeding themselves, using the potty, etc., but they are not earning love by doing those things. The mother's love for her child was always unconditional.

The difference is that our love as parents still sometimes falls short, whereas God's unconditional love is perfect.

Romans goes on to tell us that nothing can separate us from the love of God: 'For I am convinced that neither death nor life, neither angels nor demons, neither the present nor the future, nor any powers, neither height nor depth, nor anything else in all creation [and perhaps here we could include frailty and dementia], will be able to separate us from the love of God that is in Christ Jesus our Lord.'[17]

WE ARE RELATIONAL

Human beings are created for relationship. The second chapter of the Bible tells us that it's not good for man to be alone.[18]

Humans are created for relationship with God and with others: we were created to love and be loved. We only need look at the prevalence and effects of loneliness in our society today to realise this truth. Research has shown that loneliness is as harmful to our health as smoking 15 cigarettes a day![19]

We're not created to be alone; we're created for relationship. Loneliness can affect anyone, at any stage of life. But people in the fourth age of life are particularly at risk, as they may experience so much loss: of loved ones, mobility, health. Not only can they potentially have a smaller circle of meaningful relationships, they may also lack the ability to get out and about to meet people. And if they're experiencing hearing loss or visual impairment, even vintage modes of communication such as phone calls and letter writing can be a challenge. A recent study revealed that 49 per cent of older people say that the TV or pets are their main company.[20]

So, as human beings we are dependent, we are created in the image of God, we are loved, and we are relational. All these truths remain constant throughout our lives – they are not dependent on our cognition or ability; they are who God has made us to be. A frail old lady with dementia in a care home is still created in the image of God, is still loved and is still in need of relationship.

How do these truths translate into practice? How can we make sure our churches and communities are great places to grow old? Our attitude, the way we view older people, determines the authenticity of our actions and whether the church is a good place to grow old. The truths discussed in this chapter are the foundation on which we can build. Viewing and valuing older people in the way God does distinguishes us from the rest of the world and provides the motivation to action. In the next chapter we'll explore three actions out of which everything else that we do should flow.

CHAPTER 2

LOOK, LISTEN, LOVE

M istakes are great teachers, and I have made many. Even as a young student I was passionate about reaching out to older people and helped to start a Sunday afternoon service for seniors at a large charismatic church I attended. We ran it monthly, and lots of older people came. We provided transport from local sheltered housing facilities, sang old hymns and ate afternoon tea. In my zeal I decided that it would be a great idea to run an Alpha course geared up to older people and so the invitation was extended to all those who came to Sunday Afternoon at Central Hall. The morning of the Alpha course arrived, cakes had been made, the kettles were on, and nobody came. No one. My team of helpers, all senior citizens themselves, were wonderfully supportive and encouraging, as I faced a significant lesson in embracing failure. I've learnt a lot since then, not least that failure is OK and all part of the journey: it keeps you humble and often it's a first step in getting things right (unless, of course, you fail at sky diving!).

So, I want to share some of the principles I have learnt along the way about starting a new ministry amongst older people, and they build on the foundations of the previous chapter. The principles are simple: look, listen and love. If you do these things, and do them well, hopefully you will make a few less mistakes than I have.

LOOK

Before you jump into any new activity for seniors, take some time to look. Where and who are the seniors that you are seeking to serve? We need to be intentional about looking, particularly for people in the fourth age of life and carers, because they won't necessarily be around on a Sunday morning, and out of sight can often mean out of mind. Some older people may be housebound, others might be living in care homes. Make sure local care homes and sheltered housing facilities are on your radar. Here's an overview of the specialised housing for older people available in the UK.

DIFFERENT TYPES OF HOUSING AND CARE FOR OLDER PEOPLE

Sheltered housing and retirement living

Sheltered housing consists of small, individual flats equipped with a kitchen, a bathroom, and often an alarm cord or care line, where older people can live independently, but call for assistance in an emergency. Most places have some communal facilities, such as a lounge area and a warden or manager, who is unlikely to live on site, but is either there during the day or visits regularly. Places range from facilities owned and managed by local authorities and housing associations, where flats are rented, to high-end private flats that are owner occupied.

Sheltered housing and retirement living flats can be open to people over 55, some of whom are still working, so the age range and support needs of residents varies enormously. My experience of working with sheltered housing, to provide activities that encouraged residents to socialise, highlighted to

25

me that loneliness was a big issue for some residents. Younger residents, who were still fully mobile and able to work or go out, were less interested in activities that were run in the communal areas, so that events were often poorly attended. This resulted in the less mobile residents, some who had been there for many years and grown frailer over time, becoming more isolated. This was not an issue in recently built, privately owned facilities, where all the occupiers were new and keen to build community.

Extra care, housing with care and retirement villages

This is a more recent innovation in housing for older people, which generally still consists of fully equipped individual flats, but has carers available for those needing assistance with daily living. Communal areas may include a kitchen, or restaurant-type area where food is available, as well as a lounge and other services, such as a hairdresser. Large retirement villages are likely to have even more leisure facilities.

Several years ago my neighbour had a stroke which left her paralysed on one side of her body. After a short, difficult period at home, she moved to a care home for rehabilitation and eventually to an extra care scheme, which she really loved. She had her own space and independence with carers on hand when she needed them, so that she felt much less anxious than when she had been trying to live at her previous home. There were also activities organised in the communal lounge area, which she enjoyed attending, and lunches she could buy if she wasn't in the mood for cooking. However, as her health and mobility deteriorated, she eventually had to move to a nursing home.

Care homes

There are various types of care homes which offer different levels of provision: residential care homes give support in daily living and personal care; nursing homes provide additional nursing care, and dementia homes cater for people with additional needs arising from their dementia. However, the reality is not always as clear cut. Large care homes may offer a range of provision with residential, nursing and dementia care in separate units. The needs of individuals in residential care have become more complex over recent years, as people are living longer, and many have been enabled to stay in their own homes, so that those moving into residential care tend to be older and frailer than in previous generations. If someone who has been in residential care develops nursing needs or dementia, many residential homes will try to enable them to stay in familiar surroundings, with support from district nurses and other professionals, rather than undergoing the upheaval of moving to a nursing home or dementia specialist facility. However, this is not always possible.

Most modern care homes will provide individual rooms with en suite facilities, as well as communal lounge areas and social activities. Care homes can vary in size and the facilities they offer, but all in England are registered with the Care Quality Commission, who inspect them regularly, with similar regulatory bodies in Wales, Scotland and Northern Ireland.

It's a good idea to map out the accommodation that is specially built for older people in your area. The internet is full of useful websites to help.[1]

ACTIVELY RETIRED PEOPLE

Not all over 65s are frail, or even consider themselves old. My mum and dad are in their mid-70s. They have been faithful Christians since their youth, and continue to serve in a local church, always asking God what the next thing is He has for them. I asked them if they considered themselves seniors and my dad retorted, 'Certainly not!' My mum commented that she had twice been to a church seniors' group and found it soul destroying, as she's just not into activities like bingo. (Personally, I love a good game of bingo, it has so many memories attached to it of fun seaside holidays with grandparents, but clearly this passion skipped my mum's generation!) She had attempted to sit down in the circle and was firmly told, 'You can't sit there, that's Ethel's place!' She tried to sit somewhere else and was again chastised, 'That's where George sits!' Fortunately, she has a good sense of humour so teasingly asked where they would like her to sit, but if she had possessed any desire to join the group it would have been quickly vanquished.

In the previous chapter a distinction was made between the third and fourth age – the actively retired and those for whom age has brought frailty, ill-health and challenges to living independently. These are of course arbitrary differences, since the boundaries between the third and fourth age are not as impermeable as they may seem: people can move temporarily between the two during periods of illness.

However, these distinctions do hint at a gulf that may be evidenced between over 65s willing to engage in seniors' activities and those who do not identify with any older age-related categorisations. I asked my mum and dad what age label they would be happy to give themselves. Mum says she sees herself as 'young at heart' and Dad said he would just say he was in his 70s. I asked what they thought about being labelled as 'actively retired', and they were both happy with that (although Dad jokingly remarked that he'd rather be 'inactive and retired', but Mum won't let him!).

How, then, do we engage the younger old without reinforcing ageing stereotypes? Should we even be looking to engage with them as part of our ministry amongst seniors? My mum and dad see their role at this stage of life much more in serving others, rather than being served themselves, and recognise they are blessed with good mental and physical health. The main things they felt they wanted from the church were opportunities to serve in a meaningful way, and for people to listen to what they have to say. People don't have to agree with them, but they don't want to be ignored.

AfterWorkNet, a resource established by CARE to help actively retired Christians live life to the full, does not view them as 'seniors', which would resonate with my parents. In this context its programme director, Peter Meadows, reminds church leaders:

> If your church has a ministry to seniors, this is not going to meet the needs of those now retired and active. They may be willing to serve in that setting – but that's another story ... Today's retirees would most probably rather be anywhere else than counted to be among a group now designated as 'old' ... Rather, they are looking for meaningful experiences among those as alive, energetic and outward looking as themselves.[2]

I can almost hear my parents echoing an amen.

But many will still need help to adjust to retirement, to understand what fullness of life looks like after work and what discipleship means in this new phase of life. AfterWorkNet suggests eight actions that church leaders can take to support the actively retired:

1. Look out for those heading for retirement and spend an hour with them so that they feel valued and supported as they navigate this new season of their lives.
2. Treat them as a distinct church segment.

3. Encourage the activities they need, including spending time with their peers; addressing relevant issues such as loss of status; and developing a buddy system.
4. Have realistic expectations about the time they have available.
5. Don't use them – develop them. They need opportunities to grow spiritually and practically, so rather than using them as rota fodder, discover their gifts and abilities, and consider how these could open up new opportunities for the life and ministry of the church.
6. Encourage them to be salt and light.
7. Help them to reach their peers.
8. Think intergenerationally.

AfterWorkNet suggest ideas of activities to enable actively retired people to engage with their peers including a 'Let's Meet' week where various people host a coffee morning or similar, and two or three share some of the joys and struggles of post-work life as a catalyst for discussion. AfterWorkNet also have a comprehensive and practical website, along with an active Facebook group where people can engage with others and share ideas.

WHAT ELSE IS HAPPENING IN YOUR COMMUNITY?

Once you've looked for the older people, in both the third and fourth age, take some time to look at what else is happening in your community for the age group you are seeking to serve. What other organisations are out there, and what services do they provide? Map out what other organisations and churches are doing and look for where the gaps are. The internet, local libraries, community centres and council websites are great resources for this sort of mapping exercise. There's no point starting a games group on a Thursday afternoon if another popular activity is already happening at that time. But more than that, as you develop connections with other like-minded people you may find ways in which you can work together.

Another thing to look for is good practice. There is no point in reinventing the wheel: what's been done in other places that you can learn from? In later chapters we'll be exploring lots of examples of good practice, which should be a helpful starting point.

LOOK
1. Where and who are the older people you are seeking to serve?
2. What's already available to them in the local community from other organisations and churches?
3. Where are the gaps in provision?
4. What good practice examples can you learn from?

LISTEN

When you have looked for the older people you are seeking to serve, talk to them. That almost sounds too obvious to be said, but so often I see well-intentioned, enthusiastic pioneers who have a good idea, such as, 'We want to start an activity for people with dementia.' They jump right into the planning stage when they haven't intentionally chatted to a range of people living with dementia and their carers to find out what they would like. Don't assume, firstly, that older people are needy (many aren't) and secondly, don't assume what their needs are – ask older people and listen to their response.

I came across a helpful tool recently that you could use to assist in your understanding of the perspective of an older person. It's adapted from an IT project management 'user story template'. I have given five examples of people you might like to listen to, and I am sure you could add plenty more.

If you use a tool like this, it's vital that it doesn't become a form-filling exercise, which can come across as impersonal and cold. The idea is to complete it having listened to the people you are serving, not making assumptions on their behalf. Ensure people feel involved and listened to.

As a/an...	I want to....	So that...
Older member of of the church who is hard of hearing	Fully participate in Sunday services as an integrated member of the church without being in discomfort or unable to hear	I might be edified and built up through giving to, and receiving from, the church – and that the body might also benefit from my participation
Actively retired member of the church		
The wife and carer of my husband with advanced dementia		
Resident of a local care home		
Housebound member of the church who is no longer able to get to meetings		

It's also worth seeking out people from your local area who work with seniors and asking them if they have identified areas of unmet need, such as social workers and staff from local charities. Listen to their concerns and advice.

In the midst of all this, make sure you are also listening to God for the small whispers of what He might be saying. As you feel His prompting and nudging, share your thoughts with others and listen to their response. Solomon offers us some great wisdom in this area: 'Plans fail for lack of counsel, but with many advisors they succeed.'[3]

LOVE

In the previous chapter we talked about the fact that older people are deeply loved by their heavenly Father, and that if we are going to reach out in love, we too need to grasp how much we are loved, so that we give from the overflow of love that God has put in our own hearts. But how do we show that love? Well, love is practical: it is expressed in word and deed.

Paul gives us a great description of the nature of love:

> Love is patient, love is kind ... It does not dishonour others, it is not self-seeking, it is not easily angered ... It always protects, always trusts, always hopes, always perseveres ...[4]

Everything we do needs to be saturated with that patience, kindness and honouring. Love might mean sitting and chatting for an hour with someone who is feeling lonely, or helping someone who is struggling physically with their shopping, or giving them a lift to church. It might mean sitting with someone who has dementia during a church service, or starting a group where older people get the opportunity to build relationships with others. The list is endless, and you will find lots of practical examples later in this book. The point is whatever we do needs to be motivated by and done with love, expressed through kindness, patience and dignity.

Love is also expressed in our words; speaking encouragement into people's lives. It might be reminding older people that they are still loved, that they are still a valued son or daughter of the King of kings. It could be that as fourth-agers move into more dependency, we can remind them that we are all dependent and let them know what a privilege it is to be able to help carry their burdens.

As we offer unconditional love to older people, particularly those society has overlooked and ignored, we're a powerful prophetic picture of the unconditional love of God. We are loving, not for what people can give us in return, but because people are created in the image of God and deeply loved by him. How did Jesus say that the world would know that we are His disciples? Not by how much we prayed, read the Bible or ran great church events. No. It is by the love we have for one another![5]

Across the generations

I was sitting in a restaurant, more than 20 years ago, on a date with my husband, when a group of about a dozen people came in and sat at the tables opposite us. I was fascinated by them, as they were such a mixed bunch – different nationalities, cultures and ages, all having a really great time together. I wondered what common interest had brought this disparate group together and I said to my husband, 'I bet they're Christians!' And they were.

There is something powerfully distinct about togetherness. Diversity in unity. Yet so often we want to divide and segregate. We have our children's ministry, our youth ministry, our seniors' ministry – all of which are vital and valid, but often they do very little to bring the generations together. The Church is meant to be a family, the most natural multi-age community on earth, that loves and connects across the generations! We all know there's no such thing as a perfect family, but let's just imagine for a minute how an ideal family might function:

- They spend time together – whether it's doing boring stuff, fun activities or just being together.
- Everyone learns from each other – a child learning to share, or taught by a grandmother how to knit or bake cakes; children showing grandparents how to use the latest digital devices.
- They are generous with one another – they love to give. Whether it is a child drawing a picture for an adult family member; an adult giving a more expensive gift; or parents leaving an inheritance for their family.

I am sure there is much more that could be added to that list. That is what a community that loves and honours across the generations looks like. And that is what the Church should look like: spending time together across the generations, learning from each other and giving generously to one another.

Let's not be tempted to segregate our ministry amongst older people into another age-related silo but rather think about how we can also bring connections across the generations. I heard of a church recently who intentionally partner their young people with an older member of their congregation.

Recently my daughter returned from a camp of 1,400 university students involved in the leadership of their Christian Unions. She told me how one evening, instead of the usual speaker, three Christians in their 80s were interviewed on the main stage, to give advice to the students about remaining steadfast in God and passionate for His kingdom in the long haul. They offered to chat and pray with students afterwards, and after 30 minutes there was still a queue of students waiting to speak to them. At the end of the camp my daughter's group were sharing their highlights, and a large proportion said it had been hearing wisdom from the older generations! We need each other. Our church family needs the richness that all the different age groups bring. As we go on to explore different activities and models for ministry amongst older people, we will also consider ideas to promote intergenerational connections.

So, we need to look, listen and love, seeking to bring connections across the generations as we do so. One final thought before we start looking at a myriad of practical examples. What is the goal or vision for our ministry amongst seniors?

LATER LIFE IN ALL ITS FULLNESS

Jesus tells us in the Gospel of John:

> A thief comes to steal and kill and destroy, but I have come to give life – life in all its fullness.[6]

This verse was the inspiration behind the strapline for the Christian charity I founded, Embracing Age: 'Later life in all its fullness'. Recently I've been meditating on what it actually means: what is the fullness of life that Jesus intends for us, that He came to give us? Sometimes it seems that old age is like the thief who comes to rob us of our youth, our energy, our health; to kill our joy and happiness; and destroy our wellbeing. Yet, Jesus' promise of abundant life is directed to all, young and old alike. What then are the hallmarks of life in all its fullness? As I've been thinking about this, three elements come to mind: peace, purpose and pleasure.

PEACE

Peace is so much more than the absence of conflict. The Hebrew concept of peace, shalom, derives from a word associated with wholeness and completeness, and conveys all-round wellbeing, prosperity and security. The psalmist declares: 'The LORD gives strength to his people; the Lord blesses his people with [shalom].'[7] Jesus, the Prince of Shalom, tells His disciples that such peace is found in Him,[8] and it is part of the fruit of the Spirit in the lives of believers.[9] This peace, shalom, is part of the fullness of life that God intends for us; His desire is that we experience it throughout our lives, even into the fourth age, as we trust in Him. And He has given us precious promises to hold on to as we get older:

> Even to your old age and grey hairs I am he, I am he who will sustain you. I have made you and I will carry you; I will sustain you and I will rescue you.[10]

As we trust God to uphold and sustain us in our later years, He promises to give us His peace:

> You will keep in perfect [shalom] those whose minds are steadfast, because they trust in you.[11]

This shalom, this wholeness, is part of the fullness of life that God intends for believers.

PURPOSE

The Westminster Shorter Catechism states, 'Man's chief end is to glorify God, and to enjoy him forever.' The highest purpose of our lives is to glorify the Father as we walk as a son or daughter of the King of kings. Old age and frailty do not change that purpose, though it may be expressed in different ways as we experience the limitations of the fourth age.

Within the context of this highest calling, God also has other plans and purposes for our lives that never usurp our chief end, but bring us hope and fulfilment along life's journey. Many people view old age as the winter of life, but I think much of it is the autumn: a time of fruitfulness.

Psalm 92:12–14 says:

The righteous will flourish like a palm tree, they will grow like a cedar of Lebanon; planted in the house of the LORD, they will flourish in the courts of our God. *They will still bear fruit in old age, they will stay fresh and green* ...[12]

Our later years can be a time of fruitfulness as we use the time we have to serve others, the wisdom life's lessons have given us to encourage others, and – if we are fortunate enough to have wealth – to use that to bless others, as we seek to make the world a better place. Jesus tells us that the secret to a fruitful life, whatever our age, is to stay connected to Him, the vine.[13]

So, life in all its fullness includes a peace, or shalom, that passes understanding,[14] and purposeful, fruitful living. Alongside these, God delights to bring us pleasure.

PLEASURE

Did you know that God 'richly provides us with everything for our enjoyment'?[15] Not only are we meant to enjoy God forever, we are created to experience pleasure from all the gifts that He generously gives us. The gifts of friendship, love, music, nature, food, knowledge, to name a few, can all bring us joy. Even people in the advanced stages of dementia can experience pleasure and enjoyment, but more on that in the next chapter.

When Billy Graham was 94 years old, he wrote:

Life is seldom easy as we grow older, but old age has its special joys – the joy of time with family and friends, the joy of freedom from responsibilities we once had, the joy of savouring the little things we once overlooked. But most of all, as we learn to trust every day into His hands, the golden years can be a time of growing closer to Christ. And that is life's greatest joy.[16]

The point I am trying to make is that God has made it possible, through Jesus, to experience life in all its fullness throughout the course of our lives, including into our later years, and this involves peace that passes understanding, a sense of hope and purpose, and joy. Keep this big picture in mind when you are considering the purpose of any ministry amongst older people. Your vision is not just to reduce loneliness, improve health and fitness, facilitate new friendships, etc. (although all these outcomes are good and worthwhile), but to help older people know and experience life in all its fullness, available to them through Jesus.

CHAPTER 3

DEMENTIA

Before looking at practical examples of activities for seniors, it's worth pausing for a moment to consider the subject of dementia. It's the most feared illness in the over 50 age group, which isn't surprising since 1 in 14 people over the age of 65 and 1 in 6 over the age of 80 are at risk of developing it. As people are living longer, the incidence of dementia is increasing: 850,000 people in the UK are estimated to be living with dementia, and this is predicted to rise to 1.6 million by 2040. The Alzheimer's Society estimate that a new person develops dementia every three minutes![1] If you're involved in ministry amongst seniors, you are very likely to be coming alongside people living with dementia, and their loved ones. You may even decide that this is an area that your church wants to offer particular support, with a memory café or something similar.

Most people these days know at least one person with dementia, but it's worth bearing in mind a common saying in dementia circles: 'When you've met one person with dementia, you've met one person with dementia!' This emphasises that each person's journey with dementia is different, depending on which areas of their brain have been affected and their own unique response, so we therefore shouldn't generalise or make sweeping statements about the experience of dementia.

WHAT IS DEMENTIA?

Dementia is actually an umbrella term used to describe a collection of symptoms caused by diseases of the brain, including memory loss, problems with perception, coordination, reasoning and communication. There are many causes of dementia, the two most common being Alzheimer's disease and vascular dementia, where a disruption of the blood flow to the brain causes irreversible damage. Often people with dementia in later life will have a mixed condition, in other words, more than one pathological cause of brain damage which is producing their particular symptoms. Dementia is a progressive illness, which means that brain function will deteriorate as the disease progresses, causing symptoms to worsen, but the rate of deterioration will vary from person to person, depending on the cause.

Everyone's journey with dementia will be different, depending on a range of factors, not least being the combination of the areas of the brain that have been affected by the disease as we saw above.

Memory loss is perhaps the symptom most commonly associated with dementia, but it is by no means the only area of brain function affected. I recall one lady with dementia explaining how she went out for a meal with family members, and could see the knife and fork in front of her, but she just couldn't work out how she was meant to use them. These and other problems with coordination and sequencing are not uncommon, and can understandably lead to agitation and anxiety.

There are several analogies used to describe the lived experience of dementia. Some describe it as a fog that descends on bad days, whereas on good days the sun is shining and everything is clearer.[2] Perhaps the most well-known analogy for understanding memory loss in dementia is that of the bookcase, originated by Dr Gemma Jones in 2004[3] and modified for wider use by Dementia Friends. Put simply, the brain is described as having a bookcase on one side filled with factual memories, the earliest childhood memories stored on the lowest shelf, and filling up from the bottom, with the most recent memories on the top shelf. Dementia rocks the bookcase so that the books at the top are the first to fall off, which explains why people with dementia may be able to remember events that happened many years ago but may forget recent events. Each factual memory has a linked emotional memory which is stored on a corresponding shelf in a bookcase on the other side of the brain. Whereas the bookcase storing the factual memories is made of flimsy plywood, and very susceptible to the rocking of dementia, the emotional memory bookcase is built from solid oak. Dementia also rocks this bookcase, but because it is strong, the books do not fall off so easily. The point being made is that although people with dementia may forget the facts relatively quickly, the feelings will remain for longer.

This was brought home to me during the early days of visiting a care home resident. Delia has advanced dementia and lives in a specialised unit at a local care home, which is locked for the safety of the residents. I was introduced to her on my first day volunteering at the care home, and she proceeded to complain to the activity coordinator, who was with me, about various things that were frustrating her. I was just standing there, trying to look friendly and smiling, when she suddenly turned to me and growled, 'What are you laughing at? Do you think this is funny?' Needless to say, I avoided Delia on my subsequent visits to the care home and spent time instead with other residents, but I would often hear her walking to the nurses' station and shouting at the staff.

Then I attended some specialised training on how to validate people with dementia. The trainer explained that sometimes people with dementia can get very angry, and I affirmed that I knew someone like that, and avoided her because she was scary. The trainer challenged me that now I had completed this training, I was the one person who could make a difference in her life. I accepted the challenge, and the following week, as I stepped out of the lift on to the unit, I saw her determinedly heading towards the nurses' station for her usual barrage. I light-heartedly commented that she was getting some good exercise and to my surprise she smiled at me! That was to be the start of a lovely relationship, and I visited Delia regularly until coronavirus lockdown restrictions were imposed. I found out that she loves the outdoors and nature, and used to spend all her free time cycling along the local river and feeding the swans. Here she was on a locked first floor unit, with no direct access to the outside. There have been many a time when I have wanted to take Delia out to the garden, but sadly her dementia means that she also gets very anxious with the unfamiliar and isn't keen to go. On the rare days I have been able to take her out to the garden she has loved it.

I've been visiting Delia for three years and she still doesn't know my name, and she doesn't remember what we do each week. However, even in the early days I can recall her waking up as I entered her room with a look of daggers in her eyes, as if she was about to have one of her angry outbursts, but as soon as she recognised me, the anger literally melted. She doesn't know who I am, or what we do together, but she remembers the feelings I leave her with, and she associates me with those positive emotions. The factual memories seem to fall off her bookcase at a fast rate, but the emotional memories prevail.

LIVING WITH DEMENTIA

Attitudes towards dementia have progressed a huge amount in the last ten years, spurred on by the Prime Minister's Dementia Challenge in 2012 and subsequent responses, including the Dementia Friends initiative. The stigma associated with dementia has decreased and there have been many innovations in care and support to improve the quality of life for people living with dementia, particularly those in the early stages of the disease. People are beginning to realise that it is possible to live well with dementia and still have a good quality of life. I was thrilled when a retired gentleman, who volunteered in a local care home, reflected, 'I'm not afraid of dementia anymore.' Whilst volunteering he had observed that residents with dementia were still able to participate in activities and enjoy life.

Dr Jennifer Bute, a Christian GP who was diagnosed with early onset Alzheimer's, views her disease as a glorious opportunity to experience dementia from the inside and so help society understand it, and come alongside others who are living with it. She has a website full of great resources, www. gloriousopportunity.org and has written an excellent book.[4]

It would be blinkered to paint a positive picture of dementia without acknowledging that for many people the experience of dementia is a daily struggle. I think of Delia and her fellow residents on the dementia unit I visit, where invariably each week at least one resident will ask me if I can help them go home. There can be challenges too for relatives supporting a loved one with dementia, which we'll explore in more detail in the following chapter. So how can we come alongside and support a person living with dementia? We'll explore adaptations to the church environment in Chapter 6 and focus now on the needs of the individuals.

SUPPORTING PEOPLE WITH DEMENTIA

Tom Kitwood, a pioneer in person-centred dementia care, highlighted universal psychological needs that can be heightened for people living with dementia, and easily overlooked in the context of institutionalised care. They are needs we can perhaps all identify with: identity; attachment; inclusion; comfort and occupation, all held together by love, as shown in Figure 1. If I'm feeling bored I'll find something to do, if I'm feeling insecure or unloved I might seek out a hug, but people living with dementia may lack the capacity to take the initiative in having these needs met, so may express their frustration and lack in other, less obvious ways. For example, a care home resident asking if they can go home may be expressing a need for comfort, or attachment. Just as the petals of a flower often overlap, so these needs overlap and do not have distinct boundaries. Understanding these psychological needs can help us come alongside people living with dementia.

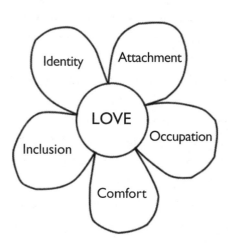

Identity: knowing who we are and what makes us unique.

Attachment: feeling connected to someone or something familiar.

Occupation: finding fulfilment in the activities of everyday life

Comfort: feeling the warmth, closeness and tenderness of others.

Inclusion: a sense of belonging in a group, feeling involved with others.

Figure 1: Flower of Need (Tom Kitwood, 1997) [5]

IDENTITY

Auguste Deter, the first person to be diagnosed with Alzheimer's disease by Dr Alois Alzheimer in the early 1900s, insightfully repeated, 'I have lost myself', when struggling to answer questions. This loss of identity was brought home to me during one of my visits to Delia, when she was feeling agitated and lamenting that she couldn't remember who she was anymore. Over the months of visiting Delia I had put together some of her life story, rather like fitting together the pieces of a jigsaw puzzle. At one point she mentioned to me that her mother and father were a Lord and Lady, and through the power of Google I was able to find photos of her family, including some wonderful portraits in the archives of the National Portrait Gallery. I had printed them and created a life story book for her. There are still many pieces of the jigsaw missing, but one of her favourite activities every week is to look at the photos. Even as her dementia has progressed she still recognises the family members in these photos, so when she was disturbed by the loss of her identity I was able to gently suggest that we look at the photos together, to remind her of who she is. Very quickly her agitation and low mood were lifted as she became absorbed in familiar photographs.

If you are walking alongside people in the early stages of their dementia journey it's so worthwhile to put together a life story book with them, including anecdotes, photos and pictures that remind them of who they are. This can be invaluable as the dementia progresses and their loss of identity becomes more acute, especially if the individual has to move into a care home, where the staff will not have known them in their pre-dementia days. The process of creating a book together can itself be a meaningful activity that provides occupation and comfort.

Knowing someone's life story makes connecting and facilitating meaningful activity so much easier. I found out very early on that

Delia loves nature, particularly trees and swans, so in the initial days of visiting, before I knew anything of her life story, I would print off swan photos and beautiful tree scenes and use them to connect with her and start the conversation. If I had just asked her direct questions about her life, she would not have been able to answer, but using prompts opened up memories that she was then able to share.

Inclusion

It's so important that people with dementia are enabled to continue with the groups and activities they enjoy for as long as possible. This may mean offering extra support, updating our facilities to be dementia friendly and adapting the way we do things.

A beautiful lady in our church, who has been a faithful member for decades, was diagnosed with atypical Alzheimer's a number of years ago, and it became more pronounced following the death of her husband. The dementia has impacted her hearing and vision, and her mobility is deteriorating. Her children help to look after her and drop her to church on a Sunday and to activities during the week, and a loyal friend always sits with her during the service and midweek activities. When I first started helping with one of the midweek groups, I was struck by how loving and welcoming she is towards others. Despite her profound deafness and other difficulties, she would walk around the group and greet people with a genuine love and interest in them.

At the lunch club she has one-to-one support because her visual impairment means she can't easily distinguish the plate and the food. The helpers ensure that she has a bright-coloured cup to drink from, so that it is something she can see and hold (a glass of water would be invisible to her) and a plate with a lipped edge. If food needs cutting, this is done in the kitchen before it is presented to her, to preserve her dignity. As her dementia has progressed she is becoming increasingly confused and also finds it more difficult to get up and walk around. It's not unusual for her to start crying, often in frustration that she cannot hear, despite everyone's best efforts to speak loudly. One week I was facilitating a small discussion group at a seniors' group, which she regularly attends. I sat next to her and held her hand throughout the discussion to bring reassurance and comfort, which seemed to help, as she remained settled. We had a time of prayer at the end and as we offered to pray for one another her tears flowed, and she cried about how much she loved everyone and just wanted to be able to help them. She so wanted to express the love she felt for people and mourned the loss that prevented her from being the help and support to others that she longed to be.

Postscript: A few weeks after writing this chapter, this precious lady died and I was privileged to attend her funeral. I had only known her latterly, during the time her dementia had become more advanced, but I was so struck by how she was described at the funeral as a lady who loved people and always gave a warm welcome and came alongside them. These aspects of her personality had shone through despite the disease.

OCCUPATION

Feeling that we are able to participate in meaningful activity is so important. Christine is an amazing lady who spent most of her life in church leadership serving others, and now has dementia and lives in a care home. Her husband, John, visits every day and once, when he asked how she was, she declared, in a rare lucid moment, that she was so bored! You'll hear more of John and Christine's story in the next chapter, but this little interaction highlights the need for occupation, for meaningful activity, and what constitutes this will vary from person to person. The lady with dementia in our seniors' group seems most engaged when she is singing old hymns or connecting with individuals. Singing and music can be powerful ways of engaging people in meaningful activity, but they are not for everybody. A memory café at a local church concluded the morning with a time of singing old songs. One gentleman could take or leave the singing and found it difficult to engage in conversation, but was brilliant at jigsaw puzzles and would spend the whole morning focused on putting one together, with other people also getting involved.

ACTIVITY IDEAS FOR PEOPLE WITH DEMENTIA

Jigsaw puzzles
Looking at photos and pictures
    of interest
Going for a walk
Singing/music
Dancing
Reading aloud
Poetry
Crafts
Art
Life story books
Word games, e.g. word search
Number games
Litter picking
Balloon and soft ball games
Hand massage
Reminiscence
Games, e.g. dominoes
Reviving hobbies, e.g. model
    building, stamp collecting
Gardening
Animals

There are so many activities that may be meaningful for people with dementia that we can help to facilitate. It could be as simple as going for a walk, or as complicated as cycling in tandem on a specially adapted bicycle. A new activity that I came across recently enjoyed by a care home resident was going out with a volunteer and litter-picking using her grabber stick. She felt a real sense of accomplishment that she was making a difference to the local environment.

COMFORT

It's hard to comprehend the confusion and anxiety that dementia can cause, especially in stressful situations. Dr Jennifer Bute[6] describes emotional 'meltdowns' triggered by tiredness, sensory overload or when things become too much, such as trying to cope with a task that is too complicated. At these times people with dementia need comfort, understanding, reassurance and sometimes distraction. Kind words, appropriate touch, a listening ear and offering a cup of tea in a peaceful environment may be the most comforting response.

When Delia becomes agitated and insists on leaving the dementia unit and going home, I find that distraction is the most effective response. I try to validate her feelings by acknowledging how much she loves her home and then I ask her to tell me about it. I try to get her talking about her garden because I know she loves nature, and then I steer the conversation on to swans, which I know bring her so much pleasure. Usually her agitation is quickly calmed as she talks and thinks about topics that she enjoys. (I should add that the care home has tried to enable Delia to live back in her own home with carers, but she became very agitated, believing the carers were intruders, so refused to let them help her, which led to disaster since she is also an insulin dependent diabetic.)

ATTACHMENT

In Chapter 1 we talked about the fact that human beings are created for relationship: we are not meant to be alone. We often sense this need for others more acutely when we are experiencing difficult situations. We want someone to be with us, reassure us, or look after us. Attachment provides security. A person living with dementia may constantly be faced with strange and anxiety-provoking situations, so the need for attachment is heightened.

Another lady at the care home where Delia lives constantly asks me if she can go home now. She will take hold of my hand and say, 'Will you help me, will you take me home?' There are so many needs she is expressing in those questions, and one of them is attachment. She is not able to hold a conversation so I can't distract her in the same way I can with Delia, so I simply walk with her, holding her hand to give her a sense of reassurance, and speak kindly to her, reminding her that this is her home now and the staff are here to look after her. For those few minutes she is reassured.

As I was reflecting on Kitwood's flower of need, and how we can support people living with dementia and their loved ones, I was reminded of some verses in Colossians:

> Therefore, as God's chosen people, holy and dearly loved, clothe yourselves with compassion, kindness, humility, gentleness and patience ... And over all these virtues put on love, which binds them all together in perfect unity.[7]

What a wonderful summary of how we can come alongside people in their journey with dementia, with compassion, kindness, humility, gentleness and patience, all wrapped up in love.

ADVANCED DEMENTIA

Dementia is a progressive disease for which there is currently no cure, which means that people living with dementia will find their symptoms deteriorating over time, along with their ability to live independently. As the disease progresses it can be tempting to withdraw, especially if you think the person is no longer there, or that they don't recognise your presence – or if you feel you may need to withdraw for your own emotional wellbeing. But, as we saw in the first chapter, people in the advanced stages of dementia are still created in the image of God, still in need of relationship and still deeply loved. They may be trapped in the depths of their dementia, but they are still there. This is powerfully demonstrated in a video on YouTube, where Naomi Feil, the founder of validation therapy, spends time with a dear lady called Gladys, who seems very locked in with her dementia, unable to talk and making repetitive movements. Yet, as Naomi connects with her through song and touch, Gladys eventually opens her eyes, joins in with the singing and even speaks a few words. It's well worth a watch, although I have somewhat given you a spoiler![8]

Not only is the person still there, they are still able to experience enjoyment, particularly through the senses, even if they are unable to participate in other activities. Touch, sound, smell, vision and taste offer a multitude of ways to connect with and bring enjoyment to people during this late stage of their dementia journey. This is particularly relevant if you are visiting people in their homes or in a care setting. Even if you don't see a response, it is worth spending time with individuals in the advanced stages of the disease, bringing enjoyment through the senses. They may be unable to communicate their response, but you are creating an environment where they feel loved, comforted, included, occupied, attached and reminded of their identity.

TOUCH

Hand massage can be a gentle way of connecting with people and bring the benefits of therapeutic touch. One of our volunteers used to visit an elderly gentleman in a care home who had been an officer in the armed forces during the war. His leg was amputated, and he was confined to a wheelchair. Each week she would give him a manicure and a hand massage, which he really enjoyed and would look forward to with eager anticipation. She asked him one week why he looked forward to it so much, and this dignified gentleman started to cry, as he explained that it was the only touch he received; it was the only time someone held his hand. If you want to learn a simple technique for giving hand massages, there is an informative video on YouTube.[9]

Touch is powerful, but it's not for everyone. I wouldn't dream of giving Delia a hand massage; she is a fiercely independent lady who has spent her life living on her own and exudes strong physical boundaries. But I always shake her hand at the end of my visit and give it a gentle squeeze, as that feels like appropriate touch for her.

A daughter learnt to give her mother, who had very advanced dementia and could not communicate verbally, gentle hand massages and found that when she finished, her mother started to massage her daughter's hand. The daughter was incredibly moved and tearfully explained that it was the first time in many years that her mum had been able to 'mother' her in any way.

Touch can bring enjoyment through different textures too, from the softness of velvet or fleece to popping bubble wrap. Individualised sensory mats and knitted twiddle muffs all serve this purpose.

I once visited a lady in a care home with very advanced dementia: she was bedbound, had visual impairment and could not speak. I asked the care home about her life but sadly, for various reasons, the staff knew very little. All I was told was her name and date of birth, so I decided to play some music from the era when she would have been a teenager, but it brought little response. I then tried to give her a hand massage but she withdrew her hand, so all I could do on that first visit was hold her hand, which she did allow me to do, and by the end of the session she was holding my hand. For the first few weeks that was all I did – try different music and hold her hand, until I eventually asked the care home for permission to phone her relatives, which they gave me. I found out that this dear lady had once been a skilled seamstress and made beautiful wedding dresses, plus I learned her favourite music and perfume. My local wedding shop donated some offcuts of beaded and lacy bridal fabric, I was able to download her favourite music to my phone and a friend donated the perfume. Each week when I visited, she would spend most of the time caressing and pulling the beaded fabric, whilst listening to music she loved and enjoying the fragrance of her favourite perfume. Sometimes she would even move her arms and legs to the music, which brings us on to the second sense, hearing.

Sound

Music is powerful and evocative, with the ability to bring life to people with dementia, and remind them of who they are. There's another great video on YouTube called Alive Inside, where a gentleman who is virtually unresponsive is played some of his favourite music through ear phones.[10] His eyes light up, he moves to the music and when people speak to him afterwards he becomes very vocal.

John Noble, who you'll read about in the following chapter, often sings old choruses and hymns with his wife, Christine, when he visits, and has videos of her joining in, even though normally she hardly talks.

Reading poetry and prose aloud is another great way to bring enjoyment through sound. Delia loves Shakespeare, particularly his sonnets, so I have broadened my literary experience as I recite them to her. Often, she is able to join in with the last few lines, which I always find so remarkable. If I am visiting people with a Christian faith or background, I find the Lord's Prayer and well-known psalms bring comfort and response.

SMELL

Smells can also evoke powerful memories and bring enjoyment. There's a certain toilet cleaner that, if I ever smell it, I'm immediately taken back to wonderful childhood holidays at a hotel we visited every year in Devon! And there are certain aftershaves that remind me of my dad. There are so many aromas we can use to bring enjoyment, whether the smell of lavender, roses or other flowers and plants, familiar hand creams, perfumes and aftershaves, and herbs or spices. I don't recommend using toilet cleaner – I think that's quite unique to me!

I visited one lady with advanced dementia at a care home who was mobile, but very unsettled and tearful a lot of the time. I took her for a walk in the care home garden and picked the lavender and rosemary for her to smell and feel, which provided temporary enjoyment and distraction for her. I couldn't solve all her problems, but that momentary enjoyment was meaningful for her, and hopefully those feelings last longer than the factual memory of what evoked them.

VISION

We have the world at our fingertips; at the touch of a button we can search the internet for just about anything and Google will reward us with an image. Pictures and photographs are great catalysts for 'in the moment' conversations that are not dependent on memory. I once had a very bizarre conversation with a care home resident with advanced dementia – she thought the care home was her private mansion and the male carer her butler, and nothing she was saying really made sense, except that she mentioned she liked a group of artists called the Canadian Five. A Google search enabled me to print off several pictures before my next visit. The following week we were able to have a very coherent discussion, looking at these pictures together. It was something in the present moment that she had thoughts and opinions about.

TASTE

A word of caution when it comes to the sense of taste. People in the advanced stages of dementia can develop problems with swallowing, and the last thing we want is someone we are visiting to choke. When we train volunteers, we do not let them give food to care home residents, due to the risk of choking and also not necessarily knowing of any special dietary requirements. But if you are the carer or loved one of a person with dementia, then you can provide tasty food and drink for them to enjoy – ice cream, jelly, smoothies, fruit – the list is endless. This not only brings enjoyment but can increase their calorie and fluid intake, reducing the risks associated with poor nutrition and dehydration.

One last story about bringing enjoyment to people in the advanced stages of dementia through the senses. I was invited by a local care home to visit a session of their sensory care programme for people with advanced dementia, where they did many of the activities listed above. I sat with a lady who was unable to speak and had painful hands, so she couldn't even enjoy a hand massage, but she liked being in the environment, with the music and the coloured lights. Then the carers brought out bubbles and started blowing them for the residents. They gave me a bottle of bubble mixture and suggested I let the lady blow the bubbles. I put the bubble stick to her lips and it was a precious moment to watch her delighted response, as she gently blew and created a stream of bubbles.

MEMORY CAFÉS

Some churches have a particular heart to reach out to people living with dementia and their loved ones. A memory café offers one opportunity to do this. A hall is set up with tables and chairs in a café style, with drinks and homemade cakes offered to guests.

Some tables have activities that people with dementia can engage with, such as jigsaw puzzles, crafts, memorabilia, colouring, etc. Carers can enjoy participating in activities or may value the opportunity to connect with other carers. Towards the end of the morning, some cafés run an activity for everyone to participate in together, such as a quiz or singing.

If your church is setting up a memory café or other activity specifically for people with dementia and their carers, volunteers should be given some training in dementia. If you are able to partner with a specialised dementia organisation such as the Alzheimer's Society to run the café, this can be beneficial. However, it's not always possible and you should not be put off if that is the case. Look for people in your church and community who have understanding and experience of dementia, who can provide wisdom and encouragement, and if possible, visit a memory café being run elsewhere to draw on their experience and advice. The vicar of St Chad's in Wembley, who set up a now well-established memory café, has written a short book which is well worth a read if you are considering this idea as a church.[11]

MEMORY CAFÉ AT ST PETER AND ST PAUL'S

Two parish churches working together in south-west London had a desire to serve people in their communities who were living with dementia by starting a monthly memory café. They talked with local organisations working in the dementia field and to people living with dementia and their carers, and visited two established memory cafés run by other churches. The church more accessible on public transport and that had a suitable and available hall was chosen to host, and volunteers were recruited from both churches and the local community.

Volunteers were given training in dementia and in providing a place of welcome, organised through a local organisation, and the launch date was set for November, to coincide with Remembrance Sunday. They meet on the first Tuesday of every month from 1.30 to 3 p.m. Volunteers arrive from around 12.45 p.m. to set up, laying the tables nicely with tablecloths and cakes (donated by volunteers). Guests arrive from around 1.30 p.m. and are offered a warm welcome. The first part of the café is chatting and socialising over a cup of tea or coffee. This is followed by a singing session and a light-hearted quiz before guests leave with any leftover cakes to enjoy at home, which they really appreciate. A pet therapy dog often visits.

They started in 2017 with four to five guests and now have ten to twelve regularly attending, and sometimes up to 19. They have been encouraged by the number of volunteers who help from the church, the local community and the nearby university. Sometimes the helpers have outnumbered the guests, but this has enabled them to offer one-to-one listening.

The feedback from guests has been positive and encouraging. The challenge remains to reach out to others who would benefit from attending, and they have tried to spread the word through posters in the local supermarket, the library, local churches and care homes. They know that transport is an issue for some people, but it is something they are unable to offer, though some volunteers do bring people they know along.

The café has evolved over time, guests and volunteers have come and gone, but the café has aimed to be a constant for the community, so that they know on the first Tuesday of each month there is a relaxed, informal, understanding and compassionate space where all are welcome.

LYRICS AND LUNCH

The benefits of music and singing for people with dementia is now well established. It stimulates the brain, brings enjoyment, is an activity that can be shared with others, and enhances quality of life. With this in mind, Jeanette Main, a primary school music teacher from Lancaster, pioneered Lyrics and Lunch, a singing and lunch group for people living with dementia and their loved ones. It combines fun, friendship, food and faith in a comfortable and relaxed setting with lots of music and laughter. Old, familiar songs are used, along with some new ones, as well as singing in rounds and playing percussion instruments to some of the songs, providing an enjoyable activity in which the person with dementia and the carer can participate together. The singing is finished with a short, dementia-friendly service, and guests stay for a nutritious lunch of soup, sandwiches, cakes and fresh fruit. Chatting with carers, Jeanette had discovered that some people living with dementia struggled to eat, and serving a healthy meal, in an atmosphere conducive to enjoying it with others, encourages them to partake. Carers are able to share stories and ideas with people who understand what they are going through and community is created for people who are feeling increasingly isolated. Faith is shared and many find great comfort in it.

Jeanette is keen to help others set up a Lyrics and Lunch group and more info about this can be found on their website.[12]

GEORGE'S STORY

In his late 80s George was diagnosed with dementia, although he had probably had it for some time. His wife had died about 15 years previously and he and his elder son had lived quietly together for most of that time. George became ill and was admitted to hospital where they also diagnosed dementia. When he returned home he was given more help and although he had become very isolated and was not keen on going out (medical appointments and a weekly visit to his other son's house were the only times he left his flat), and his granddaughter persuaded him to give Lyrics and Lunch a try. He never looked back.

George had a musical talent which had lain dormant for many years. As a young man he used to play keyboard in dance bands back in his native Scotland, even playing with some famous names such as the Alexander Brothers. At Lyrics and Lunch he loved the music and when Jeanette saw him conducting with a pen in perfect time, she decided to get him a baton and give him a job. So George became the conductor! He revelled in the attention, making jokes, doing funny movements where his baton became an imaginary violin bow and everyone grew to love him. If his taxi was a bit late and the group was waiting to start, he would enter to a round of applause, bowing and dancing in with his rollator frame, playing to the galleries! George had friends again. Lyrics and Lunch became the highlight of his week and he would practise his conducting to *Songs of Praise* on TV in-between gatherings.

In December 2017 George had his 90th birthday. He had been attending Lyrics and Lunch for nearly three years and had made a great impression on everyone with his sense of humour and fun, so a special cake was made, shaped like the accordion he used to play in his younger days and with his conductor's baton too. He was presented with a specially made picture collage of him conducting the group.

Only three weeks later George died. His health took a turn for the worse over Christmas and very early in the new year he died in his sleep. George's Lyrics and Lunch friends made his funeral a very special celebration. The team baked, catered and served the food, and the service was led by a lay reader who was part of the Lyrics and Lunch team. George's baton was woven into his coffin flowers, along with a wire treble clef. The whole funeral was an outpouring of love. The final song was one of George's favourites, 'Bring Me Sunshine', which was exactly what Lyrics and Lunch did for George and continues to do for many others like him.

DEMENTIA PREVENTION

Given that dementia is the most feared illness in the over 50s, it's no wonder that people are keen to know how it can be prevented. There is no clear cut way to prevent all dementia, as researchers are still investigating the myriad causes. The best advice is, 'What's good for the heart is good for the head!' The pathological processes that cause heart attacks are the same as those that cause strokes, trans ischaemic attacks (TIAs, or mini strokes) and vascular dementia. Most of us know what is good for the heart: healthy eating, regular exercise, maintaining a healthy weight, not smoking and limiting alcohol consumption – we're just not always very good at doing it!

Loneliness and isolation have also been linked to dementia, so it is worthwhile keeping an active social life, and treating any conditions that may lead to or exacerbate isolation, such as hearing loss and depression.

IS IT DEMENTIA?

If you are worried that someone is developing dementia, the best thing to do is to encourage them to visit their GP, and perhaps offer to accompany them. The doctor will be able to investigate the cause of the symptoms – it may not always be dementia. It could be that the individual's hearing has deteriorated, so whilst it appears they are forgetting what you have told them, they simply did not hear in the first place. Or they may have an underlying infection that is causing them to be confused. These and other causes can be effectively treated. If dementia is diagnosed, they may be able to have medication that will slow down the progression of the disease, depending on the cause, and they will be eligible for other services and support that might not be accessible without an official diagnosis.

Dementia not only impacts the life of the individual living with the disease, but also their loved ones, those journeying with them, supporting them and caring for them. In the next chapter we will explore the role of carers and how churches can support them as they juggle the responsibilities and challenges that a caring role brings.

CHAPTER 4

CARERS

I magine that someone you love suddenly, or perhaps gradually, needs caring for and the responsibility is yours. You transition from being purely a wife, husband, son, daughter or friend to a caring role, helping your loved one in ways that you had perhaps not anticipated or imagined, at a stage in life when ordinarily you may have had more freedom. Of course, caring for someone you love is a privilege, but it can also be exhausting and isolating.

Informal carers provide unpaid help and support to family and friends in need, from a few hours a week, to 24/7 provision. With the increasing crisis in social care, it is estimated that 1.4 million older people in the UK do not have access to the help and care they need, placing further burdens on informal caregivers. Roughly 1 in 8 adults are carers, the peak age being 50 to 64 years, but the proportion of carers aged over 65 is rapidly increasing, and many have long-term health needs or disabilities themselves.

Looking after a loved one can have an impact on carers. There can be financial strains from the costs associated with caring, such as equipment, laundry, heating bills and transport. These financial burdens can have a further negative effect on a carer's health, which may already be impacted from the caring role. Carers can find it difficult to find time to manage their own health, and caring can take its toll on mental wellbeing, and lead to feelings of loneliness and social isolation. The following poem, written by a carer during the COVID-19 pandemic, speaks so powerfully.

At Night by Dave

At night,
The tears often trickle down my face, in the dark.
I lay in my usual place.
My Jackie next to me.
We are together,
But separated by the night.
It should be well with my soul,
But it isn't.
It never will be now.
Though I know my God is always there.
Faithful God, so unchanging.
My secure rock, my constant Helper.
I lay my doubts, fears, and anxiety on Him.

These last months have seen change.
The pandemic has accelerated change.
I try to maintain routine,
But it is nigh impossible.
The unimagined, and daily unmanageable, merge together, then split apart.
I desperately strive to keep, and hold the tiny, individual pieces of daily living, knitted;
But they break, and splinter – every time.
A friend makes contact.
It is remote because of the virus.
It feels remote.

Each day's challenges take a little more of my being.
I am become what I do not wish to be.
A living shadow of myself.
Nearly sixty years of love continues,
And will continue, until we are parted by sweet death.

I am not afraid of death,
Though I am often frightened of living.

My faith in the Living God alone, sustains me.

We need to be intentional about seeing and supporting carers, since they may not be around on a Sunday morning due to their caring responsibilities. Out of sight can sometimes mean out of mind, adding to the loneliness and isolation carers experience. As churches we can come alongside those with a caring role and help to 'carry each other's burdens'.[1] You may decide to set up a ministry specifically aimed at supporting carers, or look to assist them and connect them with others through endeavours such as a memory café.

In this chapter we will hear the stories of two carers, both looking after a loved one with dementia, to give first-hand insight into the joys and challenges of a caring role. Then we'll explore ways in which the church can support carers as part of their ministry. Of course, people may be in a caring role for many reasons, not just in looking after someone living with dementia.

JOHN AND CHRISTINE'S STORY

John and Christine Noble were involved in Christian ministry together for almost 50 years. Married in 1958, they soon found the Holy Spirit at work in their lives as they were caught up with the charismatic renewal that emerged in the 1960s. Alongside bringing five wonderful children into the world, they planted churches, shared in great conferences like Spring Harvest and developed a team to serve the Church in the UK and around the world.

Having been trained at the Royal Academy, Christine had a passion to see the arts functioning freely in worship and the Church's mission. With her team she pioneered the use of movement, drama and art which, with a strong prophetic element, enriched Christian gatherings at every level. She was greatly used in the gifts of the Holy Spirit and saw many people delivered, healed and released into ministry. She also did much to engender self-esteem amongst women and encouraged them to pursue their God-given callings in work, home and church, in whichever way the Lord was leading them. Together, John and Christine were a great team and spent many years serving the Church, from simple tribal village fellowships in Asia and Africa, to the city churches of the West and beyond.

In 2011 Christine was diagnosed with an aggressive form of dementia and they were faced with the greatest challenge of their long and happy relationship. John was devastated and wanted everyone to know and pray for them, while Christine was inclined to be in a measure of denial. This immediately led to some tension and made it difficult to manage the inevitable adjustments the progression of the disease brought. Nothing John had been through in life had prepared him for the situation they found themselves in and he found himself on a massive learning curve.

John admits that he didn't always handle things very well as the Christine he knew seemed to fade away and a different Christine emerged. It was a Christine who didn't behave and react the way she had done in the past, and John was left coming to terms with a disturbing range of emotions, from bewilderment and confusion, to hurt, anger and sadness. If it wasn't for the support of a loving family, praying friends and a few people with experience, who listened to his pain and took time to sympathise and gently give words of counsel, John does not think he would have survived.

Two days after John's 80th birthday Christine was taken into care for a couple of weeks to sort out her medication, which wasn't working too well. It was the worst day of John's life and he wept constantly. During her short stay she was seen to be in an advanced stage of disease and the assessor said that she was amazed that they had managed to cope for so long. So Christine stayed in the home, which was both a relief and a further devastation.

Reflecting on the support he valued from the church, John writes:

As I look back I see that the very first kind of support we had from people in the church I didn't recognise as being support at the time. A couple, who were long-standing friends in our church, were brave enough to come and see us to suggest that Christine's forgetfulness might be more than just the ageing process. They advised us to get an appointment with our doctor for a referral to the memory clinic where we eventually received the diagnosis. That was very kind of them, as few people would find the courage to suggest to a friend that there may be a serious problem which they need to face up to.

It was strange, as the word 'Alzheimer's' was the one we were concerned about, but when the diagnosis came it was 'dementia'. Christine's reaction when she heard that was to say, 'Oh, good! I haven't got Alzheimer's, then!'

We then received advice and prayer from a Christian

friend we trusted in a church nearby, who was a doctor. That was very special, as he talked to us with compassion but very frankly and encouraged us to plan ahead for the inevitable. It was then that we arranged power of attorney and I was very glad to know that this issue was resolved before the disease took control.

As far as support from our small church group went, my expectations were realistic. I look back on my own reaction to people who were facing challenges way beyond anything I had experienced and apart from sympathy and prayer and trying to be there for them in their need, I didn't have a great deal by way of experience to offer. So I wasn't disappointed when that is what we received: love, empathy and concern as to how we were coping, which was as much as they could give. However, no doubt as a result of those prayers, the Lord sent along one or two key people from our wider circle of relationships who did have experience to give me input and help at just the right time.

We are fortunate to have a large family, some of whom are part of our church group or close to us, and they have been fantastic. I shudder to think how people with no church or family manage or survive with the tremendous challenges such a disease brings.

I must confess that I am a pretty independent kind of person and looking back I see that I wasn't keen to look for help or support from people I didn't know. I tended to disregard leaflets and other materials passed on by medics and societies as it all seemed a bit impersonal. Also, I felt sure that we would get through somehow and didn't take the time to look for helpful literature, or other sources of information or activities. In retrospect I realise that this was naïve and short-sighted.

However, when my daughter, Sharon, arrived to help, she began to read up about what to expect on our journey and to find out what was available. She was looking out for anything we could do to break up the daily routine and provide moments of relief. She also took on all the form-filling and admin, which was a real Godsend.

Older folk who are carers may not be familiar with the internet and struggle to find out what is going on. This is where someone who may not be competent to help with the caring side of things may be quite capable of going online to search out what is happening in the locality, or find where you can get help for any particular problems that may arise. They may also find that you are not claiming all the benefits that you are due.

With Sharon's help we found a number of activities taking place in the area which we tried out; some worked for us and others didn't. The weekly club run by a lady Methodist minister where we met others in a similar position to ourselves was great. We sang, played games, were entertained and had tea and cakes. There was also a club run by the local social carers which was similar and we were able to talk together about our experiences and challenges, which worked quite well for us.

During one of John's first visits to see Christine, he was distressed and upset. A lady who was visiting her mother took a moment to come over to him and offer kind words of comfort and encouragement. Since then, during his daily visits, he has had dozens of opportunities to do the same for other visitors who might be facing an emotional challenge with their loved one. John is keen to encourage more churches to adopt their local care home, with volunteers trained to come alongside residents, relatives and staff.

JEANNETTE AND JOHN'S STORY

Jeannette and John met at their church youth group in Croydon and kept in touch whilst John went to the University of Cambridge and Jeannette trained to be a nurse. They were eventually married in 1968, and continued to be involved in the life of a local Baptist church, supporting missionaries together and raising their two boys. When John retired they helped relaunch an Anglican church in West London, running the first Alpha course, leading a life group and playing an active part in the prayer ministry team. Jeannette describes these years as the best time of their lives. John helped to do maintenance in the church building during the day, while Jeannette was still at work. They found being part of the prayer ministry team very fulfilling, and leading Alpha groups and their life group were stimulating, as they interacted with lots of different people from all walks of life.

Eight years later Jeannette retired, but a month after this John was diagnosed with Alzheimer's disease. Jeannette felt angry at the way they were told and humiliated by the lack of compassion or empathy shown by the medical team. There was no help, information or follow-up given; they were just left to get on with things. It seemed to Jeannette that she was looking down a long, dark tunnel with no light at the end. She thought she had finished her nursing career, but realised that it would now continue in a different capacity. John was in denial; he had no interest in finding out more about the disease and felt it would make no difference. Jeannette immediately told her family and church friends, and spent a lot of time praying to come to terms with the diagnosis.

In the early stages, Jeannette tried to keep life as normal as possible, encouraging John to be active in the day-to-day running of the home, although he was relieved to let Jeannette sort out their finances, and readily agreed to power of attorney being organised. It was the last time he was able to write his name. He did not resist when he had to give up his driving licence, as he realised he might be a danger to other road users, and was happy to let Jeannette drive instead, although he would often point out hazards he thought she might have missed!

Jeannette re-joined the model railway club that John had once belonged to, but the members were not at all empathetic about his condition, despite Jeannette explaining it to them, and they would not let him work on any of the layouts. Jeannette resigned their membership and instead found models they could work on together at home. Eventually, John attended a dementia specialised day centre three days a week, which he enjoyed and which gave Jeannette some respite.

Jeannette and John's experience at church was the complete opposite to their rejection at the model railway club. Folk accepted his condition with love, compassion and support, not excluding him from conversations, even knowing that he might not reply. Although Jeannette and John had to gradually step down from being on the prayer ministry team and as life group leaders, the life group continued to meet at their house. The church gave other practical help as John's condition deteriorated: a couple would occasionally sit with him while Jeannette had an evening out, and since the wife was a nurse, Jeannette felt confident that John was in good hands. They also helped to move his bed downstairs so that John did not need to use the stairs, and Jeannette could care for him more easily.

The most difficult season for Jeannette was when John lost his mobility. Social services had organised for carers to help and the district nurses had arranged for a hospital bed, table and hoist to be delivered, along with an adjustable chair. However, Jeannette couldn't get them to organise a ramp or a wheelchair, so they were both stuck indoors for three months, with John unable to attend the day centre. It felt to Jeannette as if they were on house arrest, but their life group came to the rescue. They found out that there was a redundant ramp at the church, and asked if John and Jeannette could use it, and then brought it to their house. A neighbour then loaned a wheelchair, and John was able to go back to the day centre again.

At that point Jeannette started attending a more local church that she could take John to on the bus, in his wheelchair. Having been unable to attend a church service for a few months, John was happy to hear the songs he loved once more. Although he couldn't always participate in the singing, he enjoyed being in the presence of God and sometimes his eyes would fill with tears as he soaked in the atmosphere. Their old life group continued to come and hold meetings at John's bedside. This made him smile and he seemed to recognise them. Two kind ladies from the new church offered to take John out for walks, or sit and sing for him in the evening, which was a real encouragement to Jeannette.

After eleven and a half years journeying with dementia, John was becoming weaker and collapsing when moved with the hoist. Some of Jeannette's Christian friends had sensed that God would show her when John was to die. Jeannette had prayed that this would be in hospital, as she could not face it happening at home. During the winter he continued to attend the day centre three times a week, but shortly before Christmas he developed a cough and Jeannette was concerned he may be developing a chest infection. A doctor visited and examined John, but found nothing. That evening a friend visited to play carols for John while Jeannette attended the church carol service. As Jeannette came through the front door on her way back she heard her friend playing, 'Thine Be the Glory', which has the lyric:

Thine be the glory
Risen conquering Son

Endless is the victory
Thou o'er death has won[2]

Jeannette sensed then in her heart that the end was near. During the night John's condition got worse, so she called an ambulance and they took him to the hospital. The doctors confirmed how serious his condition was, so Jeannette was able to phone her son, who came immediately, and together they watched as John quietly slipped away. Jeannette felt relieved that John had passed away at the hospital, and that God had given her that sense of when it would happen.

I asked Jeannette how she had coped since John's passing, especially with the transition to no longer being in a caring role. This is what she said:

After John's loss of mobility, and we transferred to a local church, my son suggested I find things to do while John was at the day centre. So I started volunteering at the church lunch club. I soon made new friends. Then I started going to the Thursday Bible study group, and was invited to lead when I felt I could. They knew I might have to pull out at a moment's notice.

This meant that after John passed away, I could continue with those events. As it was Christmas time and there was still lunch to prepare for the whole family, I was able to keep busy, organising the removal of bed, chair, hoist, etc. I was also given the scripture that said, 'Your mourning will soon be over'.

One lady from the church invited me to Sunday lunch and others to have coffee which helped fill some time while I was trying to sort out finances and other paperwork. I found it helpful sorting through the photos for the Thanksgiving

Service, and remembering the thousands of happy times we had together. I will remember that service with joy and thanks to those who made it such a fitting tribute to a faithful husband, friend, father, and a lovely Christian man.

Both John and Jeannette felt supported by their church communities, but sadly that is not the experience of all carers. A research study of 50 Christian carers of persons with dementia found that whilst most received some degree of practical, pastoral or prayer support from their church, this was not universal, and in some cases was completely non-existent. Carers in the study wanted churches to have a deeper understanding of dementia and what they were going through as carers. Four key challenges were identified: loneliness; strain on health; the relentlessness of the task and the progressive decline of the person cared for.[3]

CARERS CONNECTED

Aware of some of these challenges, and seeing an opportunity afforded by the widespread use of online video platform Zoom during the pandemic, a new initiative called Carers Connected was started.[4] A weekly Zoom meeting connects Christian carers from across the UK, enabling them to chat and pray together. Carers Connected is open to all, so if you have carers in your congregation who might benefit from chatting and praying with other Christian carers, do point them in the direction of the website, where there is a wealth of information for both carers and churches.

I have the privilege of participating in these weekly Zoom meetings and was able to listen as carers were asked about the support they receive from their church. What follows are some guiding principles that emerged from those discussions.

GUIDING PRINCIPLES FOR CHURCHES IN SUPPORTING CARERS

1. PARTICIPATION AND PRESENCE VERSUS PERFORMANCE AND PERFECTION

Are our churches really places where people can come as they are, and be involved as they are, or are we in danger of creating churches for the successful? What's more important in your church, performance or participation?

Carers want the person they are caring for to feel accepted and included. We saw the two sides of this in Jeannette's story, when John was not allowed to get involved at the model railway club, but was able to participate in the life group. Let's actively look for opportunities to involve those who might otherwise be overlooked. We heard some lovely examples of this in the Carers Connected group. A lady with dementia able to help with communion by collecting the empty glasses; a retired vicar with dementia able to sing Compline for Lent; a man with learning difficulties able to do the Bible reading. It made carers happy to see their loved ones being able to take part in these meaningful activities. Church is family, and family doesn't have to be perfect. Are we a greater witness to the unconditional love of God when we put on a perfect service, or when we allow people to participate with a less than perfect performance?

2. ENABLE SERVING WITH A SAFETY NET

Carers and their loved ones might want to continue with ministries they have been involved in, but what is helpful to them is having a safety net, so that if they have to unexpectedly pull out, there are others who can step in at the last minute. Let's enable both carers and those they care for to be as active and involved as they would like to be, by surrounding them with the additional support they need to participate.

3. KEEP ASKING

Make sure carers don't get forgotten. It might be hard for them to ask for help, or even admit that help is needed. Check in regularly and find out how they are. There's a trap we can slip into of only asking after the cared for, but carers need to know that people are interested in how they are as well.

However, like most of us, carers may find it difficult to respond to the question, 'How are you?' It will depend on who is asking, where the question is posed and the level of trust felt. It's not helpful to ask this question if the carer is with the person they are caring for. They are unlikely to want to be open about challenges they are facing in front of their loved one, as they will not want to make them feel a burden. So, if you really want to know how a carer is feeling, ask them at a time and a place where they can respond openly and honestly, without feeling like they are dampening the mood of a social occasion, or being negative in front of the person they are caring for.

4. BE SPECIFIC ABOUT THE HELP YOU ARE ABLE TO PROVIDE

How often have you said to someone, 'Let me know if there is anything I can do to help'? I confess to being guilty of this. I've said it with the best of intentions, but carers have told us that they are unlikely to take up such a generalised offer. Far better to be specific: Have you got any ironing I can do for you? Would you like me to sit with your loved one for an hour or two this week so that you can have some time to do other things? Could I bring a meal round for you on Wednesday? You get the idea. If you have no clue of what might be helpful to offer, a good question to ask is, 'What would be the most helpful way for me to support you?'

5. KEEP INCLUDING

It's easy for carers to feel forgotten when they are unable to participate to the extent they would like. Make sure they are kept up to date on what is happening in the life of the church and that they are supported pastorally. One carer made a simple suggestion of churches having a regular slot on the church newsletter or website specifically aimed at supporting carers.

Alongside these guiding principles, some churches may be inspired to start specific activities to support carers.

DEMENTIA CONVERSATIONS

Dementia Conversations was started by Dementia Pathfinders,[5] to provide opportunities for carers and those living with dementia to support one another, as they share experiences together, gain knowledge and explore issues related to living with dementia. The founder, Barbara Stephens, had seen the huge benefits of people being able to share and support one another informally during difficult seasons of life. Dementia Conversations began on the Isle of Wight in partnership with a local church and is led by a skilled facilitator and a church minister.

Inspired by this model, David Jolley, a retired consultant psychiatrist, established a monthly Dementia Conversations group at his Methodist church in Bowdon Vale, with the support of the Revd Ros Watson. They advertised it in church newsletters and local papers encouraging anyone living with dementia, carers or those just interested, to come along.

They have been meeting monthly since 2016, for two hours on a Tuesday afternoon, and moved online during the pandemic. The session starts with introductions and general chat, which opens up topics for discussion, which are either explored there and then, or on another occasion to allow time for researching the issue. There is much interpersonal support during these conversations, spreading into refreshment time and beyond.

The second half usually addresses a topic identified as a particular interest or worry, with occasional visiting speakers, but mostly in-house. There is often an activity, such as singing, reading, playing records, puzzles, etc. and themed days have become a regular feature: Christmas; seaside holidays; harvest festival. These give a framework for enjoying the time together and a hint towards reminiscence and the feelings associated with people and times.

There are highlights and new learning every month as people share their stories. There are sad moments and struggles too, as they see situations and people deteriorate and change over time. A wife or husband supported strongly and optimistically at home for months and years, gradually becomes so changed and their needs so challenging, that a move into residential care becomes essential. The transition, the complexity and unfairness of funding opens up new chapters. A husband and wife, both known to have dementia, lose one partner, so life becomes solitary, transport is difficult, movement to a sheltered complex promises some additional help, but establishing a new routine takes time. They journey with people through these difficult challenges and transitions.

David offers this advice to those considering setting up a Dementia Conversations group:

Dementia Conversations gives time and space to consider and share pretty deep reflections on our condition as human beings, sometimes stressed or altered by illness. It is a sort of oasis for thought and feelings within. To offer this requires two leaders who are committed to the idea and equipped by training and knowledge to run a reliable, ethical and responsible project. They will explore the range of interests locally and find a place where the sessions can be held.

More information and guidance is available from Dementia Pathfinders.

KEYSTONE

The Keystone Project, based in Liverpool, aims to support carers and to provide a safe place for them to express their emotions honestly. It was established by Jane Stephens, who has a background in nursing, midwifery and health visiting, as she saw the toll that caring for a loved one with dementia took on her now husband, Colin. At the funeral of Colin's mum, who had Alzheimer's disease, the local vicar declared, 'What we need is a support group in the village for those caring for a loved one with dementia.' It was a light bulb moment for Jane, as she thought, 'I could do that!'

An initial group was started by the vicar that quickly folded, as volunteers were invited from the local community who came with their own agendas, and Jane was then invited to start a new group based in her church. Rather than making a general call for volunteers, she prayed about who to ask and approached people individually, asking them to pray about it before giving her an answer. The team that was formed out of this in 2013 is the same core team she has today.

Each group of carers is taken through a four to six session course that Jane has developed, which starts with each carer telling their story, and goes on to look at subjects such as: how memory works; the importance of not asking direct questions and not contradicting; how to cope with difficult behaviour;

looking after yourself as a carer; benefits and other relevant topics.

Following this course, each group has continued to meet monthly and taken on a life of its own. The carers who were part of the original group meet in one room and those they care for meet in a café on the same site, with other volunteers. Carers said very early on that they could not be honest with their loved one sitting with them. The carers ask each other how they cope with various things, and discussions inevitably follow. They talk regularly about moving to a care home and carer's guilt.

A memory café also evolved from the carers of the first group, when one carer said she would like to go out for coffee without worrying that her husband would say something out of place or be stared at. They meet at the Churches Together café where members of the public are also present.

There is a group for carers of people with early onset dementia, where adult children of the person living with dementia often come. There is also a second memory café, in a different church location and an evening group for those carers who are still working, although this is not always well attended. Keystone have recently started a regular games morning, as carers were talking about loneliness and a trial games morning proved a great success.

Alongside these groups, they hold Christian services three times a year and a carers' service on the fifth Sunday of the month, as well as social gatherings, including a Christmas lunch at the local golf club and an afternoon tea for Carers Week in June. There is also a monthly prayer meeting which mainly the team and prayer partners attend, and regular conferences.

Reflecting on the challenges of setting up and running Keystone, Jane is aware that there are some people they are unable to help, because the carers view their situation as worse than anyone else, and nothing suggested helps. Jane has found that it is the other carers who have commented on this, as they tend to be very honest in their dealings with one another. Another difficulty has been two situations where they have dealt with people with dementia who are very aggressive and for the safety of their volunteers and other carers they have reluctantly had to stop them coming. Jane has personally found it a struggle to find time for her and Colin. She tried in the past to take holidays in the weeks where there wasn't a Keystone meeting but that meant only ever being away for a week, so she has had to learn to trust other people to lead meetings.

Jane gives this advice to other churches looking to start similar projects:

1. Is there a need in your community? She went to one church and there was a group running less than 100 yards away in another church!
2. Pray for the team. Once the team is in place, get some training and only then start to advertise.
3. Don't expect a big group to start with. Start small and learn from your carers.
4. Listen to the carers and change or expand as they need or want.

RON'S STORY

Ron Savage, 94, was one of the first members of Keystone. He shares:

My wife Joan is 92 this year; she has been suffering from dementia for about 5 years and has been in residential care since July 2015. I have been coming to Keystone since it opened and my wife was still at home with me. I am the oldest and eldest standing member! I was somewhat lost after Joan was diagnosed. I found myself feeling bewildered and quite lonely. I do feel guilty at times. I question whether I have done enough for my wife. Coming here regularly has been my solace. It is a place full of love and fun. I think it's rather wonderful to have a place where we can talk our problems over. The comradery is like coming to a home from home, a lovely happy family.

MICHAEL'S STORY

Michael Stone, 81 attends the Keystone meetings. His wife has dementia and lives in a care home, after spending 18 months at home following her diagnosis, during which her health rapidly declined.

Michael reflects:

I first heard about Keystone through Ron and started coming along to the carers meetings. When I made the decision to look into residential care for my wife I was at breaking point really. I was that physically and emotionally drained that I knew I would have gone under if it had carried on much longer. I have now reached a stage where my wife is comfortable and is being well cared for, even though she won't recognise me and that I'm her husband.

Keystone has allowed me to meet and talk to other people who are going through this. They were great at the beginning in setting out basic rules about how to cope and how to talk to someone with dementia. Not to worry about having to tell a white lie in order to save upsetting or agitating the person when they will only forget about it anyway. It's this practical advice on how to handle situations that has been so valuable to me.

Suddenly you find yourself alone. You have to start living another life. I cried my eyes out when the time came for my wife to go into residential care. The GP recommended that I try counselling but no, I couldn't stand it. It doesn't work for everyone. It is a very emotional upheaval, almost like a bereavement. I am so glad for the support of Keystone.[6]

The wives of both Ron and Michael eventually moved into a care home to receive the care and support they needed. Care homes play a huge role in looking after some of the oldest and frailest people in our society. The following chapter explores how churches can come alongside care home residents.

CHAPTER 5

CARE HOMES

You may be tempted to skip this chapter, as you're keen to read on about activities for older people that can be run in church buildings. Let's pause for a moment there. Why is it that older people in care homes get passed over? I have worked in the charity sector for more than a decade and my experience has been that there's a widespread belief that as soon as someone moves into a care home they are OK. They've got carers on hand 24/7 to meet all their needs, so we don't have to worry about them anymore.

I admit to thinking similar thoughts years ago, when my neighbour, Doris, moved into a care home. She had suffered a major stroke which left her paralysed on one side and wheelchair-bound, and had carers visiting her at home four times a day. It was an awful season for Doris, as the carers had very little time to actually care and would often be running late. They were meant to be enabling and rehabilitating, but they just didn't have the time to do anything more than meet her basic needs. She was trying to adjust physically and psychologically to the limitations of the stroke, and the support she needed was not available. I would pop over and find her crying at the lack of care. One time, her lunch, which the carer had left on a tray for her to eat, had fallen on the floor and she had no way to pick it up. Numerous times she would be in bed, soaked in urine because the carer was running late, so there was no one to help her onto the toilet. I helped when and where I could, but it was a drop in the ocean compared to her needs. So, when she was moved into a care home, I felt relieved for her. She had been lonely, isolated and anxious at home, but in the care environment she would be surrounded by others. In fact, it did prove to be a good move for Doris, as she was given the rehabilitation she desperately needed, but she was still very lonely.

Research shows that elderly care home residents are twice as likely to feel severely lonely as older people in the community.[1] One resident told me, 'You can be alone in a crowd, you really can.'

This might seem surprising. But most of us, during the course of our lives, get to choose where we will live and who we will live with. When you move into a care home you may get to choose where you will live (though not always – it might just be where there is availability), but you certainly don't get to choose your living companions. Just because people are of a similar age does not mean they will have much in common. Plus, as we get older, many of us experience hearing loss or visual impairment, which can make communication more challenging and frustrate the building of relationships. Furthermore, an estimated 70 per cent to 80 per cent (depending on which report you read) of care home residents have dementia or significant memory loss. Research shows that people with dementia are more at risk of loneliness and, if you are one of the 20 per cent of residents who do not have dementia, it can be hard to build meaningful relationships in an environment where the majority of people do.

Have you ever moved to a new place and needed to start over in finding your sense of belonging and community? I remember the move to university, many years ago, leaving my established friendship group in my home town, and being thrown together with a group of strangers, in the halls of residence. I felt incredibly lonely. Of course, Freshers' Week at the university and a myriad of clubs and societies are all provided to help students mix and make friends, and if you don't get on with the people you are living with, there are always other places to meet people, and the prospect of moving out in your second year.

Not so with care home residents. Yes, some may have the option of moving, but usually this is quite an upheaval, and for most the care home will be their last place of residence.

Perhaps you have not known loneliness, but during the lockdowns of the COVID-19 pandemic we all experienced restriction to our freedom, not being able to do what we wanted when we wanted, and limitations in meeting with our friends and family. Now imagine you are faced with those prospects for the rest of your earthly life, and it might give you a small insight into the life of a care home resident. It's not that these restrictions are externally enforced, but often due to declining physical or cognitive function.

Jean, who was in her early 90s, had to move into a care home after a number of falls, because she could not manage physically at home, but she didn't feel mentally ready for the transition into a care environment. She is a very sharp lady, with no hint of dementia or memory loss, and she found the psychological adjustment to life in a care home incredibly difficult. She didn't see much of her family as they were often abroad, and she felt cut off and in need of stimulation from the outside world. She felt there were few people in the care home she could make meaningful connections with, and she couldn't get out easily on her own.

Jean explained how at one point, as she was adjusting to life in a care home, she had what she describes as a 'meltdown'.

She felt that she had no one to talk to and no one to tell. She channelled her emotional turmoil into art and painted a picture of a solitary figure on a stormy sea, with arms raised in despair. It's a powerful image that depicts her completely alone and not knowing where to turn.[2]

Some may point out that at least there are staff available 24/7 in a care facility. This is true, and care home staff certainly do an amazing job, in what is generally a low-paid position. You can get more for walking a dog than you can for looking after our older people! Low wages can lead to problems in recruitment, so that many care homes rely on agency staff to fill the gaps, staff who may not know the residents well. Care staff are usually very busy, and it's completely unrealistic to expect them to meet all the social and emotional needs of residents, as well as all their nursing and physical needs. Besides, I remember hearing one resident, who was advocating for the role of volunteers in care homes, commenting that she just wanted to be able to talk to someone who hadn't seen her naked!

There's a huge role for volunteers in care homes to come alongside, spend time and build friendships with residents. Volunteers have the time that staff simply don't, to sit and chat, or do one-to-one activities with residents, like playing a game of chess.

Of course, not every care home resident is lonely, just as not all older people living in the community experience loneliness. A care home resident, who I was chatting with about the role of volunteers in care homes, remarked, 'Well, actually, I think it's a good thing if volunteers come in and see what happens in a care home, because I think it's a good thing if they carry out the message, "Don't worry if you have to go into one, it's a good place to be." That's part of the work of volunteers… I'm glad I came.'

The question still remains, why do older people in care homes often get overlooked? Is it simply a matter of out of sight, out of mind? Perhaps. Certainly there are so many pressing needs in society for churches to attend to, like homelessness, food poverty, poor mental health, provision for young people, etc., that it's easy for care home residents to be bottom of the list, especially with the false assumption that they can't be lonely when they are surrounded by others. But I do wonder if there are also other reasons at play. After all, reaching out to care home residents is unlikely to result in numerical church growth, and won't fill slots on church rotas. It's a hidden ministry in many respects that is mostly unlikely to herald public applause. And yet, I'm reminded of the words of Jesus in Matthew 25:34-36:

> Then the King will say to those on his right, 'Come, you who are blessed by my Father; take your inheritance, the kingdom prepared for you since the creation of the world. For I was hungry and you gave me something to eat, I was thirsty and you gave me something to drink, I was a stranger and you invited me in, I needed clothes and you clothed me, I was ill and you looked after me, I was in prison and you came to visit me.'

Jesus sees the acts of kindness we do for others as ministering to Him and He is attentive to the things done in secret. He invites those who minister in this way to come and take their inheritance in the kingdom, and calls them 'blessed by [the] Father'. What higher commendation could there be?

Perhaps another reason that care home residents are largely overlooked, is the difficulty of facing our own fears about ageing, dementia and mortality. We are all getting older, and visiting care home residents opens our eyes to some of the stark challenges and suffering that old age can bring. We don't want to be dependent, or incontinent, or cognitively impaired, so subconsciously we avoid situations that remind us of these realities.

But we do not need to fear ageing. We have a heavenly Father who has promised never to leave us or forsake us.[3] And He has assured us:

> Even to your old age and grey hairs I am he, I am he who will sustain you. I have made you and I will carry you; I will sustain you and I will rescue you.[4]

My experience of visiting care home residents, and feedback from the army of volunteers we are raising up to do the same, has been that it brings so much enrichment into our lives. We make new friends, hear incredible life stories and learn new skills, as well as experiencing the joy of giving and the satisfaction of making a difference in people's lives.

My final thought on why care home residents, and perhaps older people generally, are sometimes overlooked in church contexts is our obsession with youth, and raising up the next generation. I know I might offend a few people on this point, but please hear me out! As a mother of three young adults I am totally committed to investing in younger people, and I'm so grateful for the youth leaders I had as a teenager, and for those currently inputting into the lives of my children.

We know that the population is ageing and the Church is ageing at a faster rate due to the declining numbers of young people and children. Understandably, in recent years there has been an emphasis on drawing young people back into church life and this is clearly needed, but to do so to the detriment of older folk is short-sighted, lacks authenticity and is potentially divisive.

Even with an increased number of young people, we will still have more and more older people in our congregations, as we cannot reverse the wider tide of an ageing population. Nor should we want to – an ageing population is a positive thing – we are all living longer! Many churches have youth and children's workers, but far fewer have someone assigned to their older people, let alone a strategy for discipleship in later life and for mission to the wider ageing community. Let's start investing as much in our older people, including those in care homes, as we do in the younger generations.

If you are reading this book, I'm sure I am preaching to the converted, when it comes to having a desire to invest in the lives of older people, but you may recognise in your church some of the barriers and attitudes I have outlined. And coming alongside older people in care homes may not have been at the forefront of your ideas for ministry amongst seniors.

John Noble, who shared Christine's journey with dementia in the previous chapter, feels that reaching out to care home residents is an area where the Church has dropped the ball. Visiting her daily, he sees the gaping needs and opportunities for volunteers to bring Christian love and ministry to the residents, relatives and staff. Recently I was chatting to a young man, the son of missionaries in Brazil, who had returned to England, and asked the Lord to open his eyes to the poor in the UK. The Lord showed him the poverty of spirit of care home residents and this young man felt prompted to give up his promising career in recruitment to work as a carer.

It's worth noting that care home residents are not being completely overlooked. There are a number of Christian organisations providing excellent care home facilities across the UK, and large numbers of churches that run regular services in care homes, along with countless Christians who faithfully visit residents. The message we often hear from these folk is that they see so much need, and don't know what to do or where to start to begin to address it. Hopefully the following ideas will provide good starting points.

The COVID-19 pandemic highlighted the vulnerability and isolation of care home residents. Care homes were forced to shut their doors to all visitors, meaning relatives, volunteers, clergy and others could no longer visit. As I write, care homes are beginning to open again, with restrictions and precautionary measures in place, but there is still much uncertainty.

Many of the ideas that follow have been implemented in a pre-COVID world, and will have been greatly impacted by the virus. But care homes will open up more fully at some point so this is an ideal time to reimage, pray and plan what your church's ministry to care home residents might look like.

REACHING OUT TO CARE HOME RESIDENTS

So, what can we do to reach out to care home residents with the unconditional love of God? It's worth saying at this point that we don't need to do a lot to make a huge difference. For Jean, who painted the picture of herself completely alone in a storm, a volunteer was found who could accompany her on weekly walks, and she says he absolutely transformed her life. She described it as 'being in the normal world, with normal people, talking about normal things'. Something so simple, but for Jean it made all the difference. Delia, the lady with advanced dementia I mentioned earlier who I visit weekly, often says to me at the end of my visits, 'Thank you so much for coming to see me, it's so lovely to have someone to talk to!' It's only an hour of my time each week, but for her it's the difference between having someone to talk to, or no visitors at all.

There are a number of established ministries reaching out to care home residents in different ways, which we will now explore.

EMBRACING AGE

There are about 12,000 care homes for older people across the UK and more than 50,000 churches. Imagine if each care home was adopted by a local church, with trained volunteers spending time and building friendship with residents. Even if only 1 in 4 churches got involved, we could make an enormous difference in the lives of care home residents across the nation. This is the vision of the Embracing Age project, which I set up in 2015, and we are supporting and enabling churches to raise up an army of trained volunteers to befriend residents.

This is a relatively straightforward project for a church to start. All it takes is one champion from the church who can gather a small group of volunteers. Staff from Embracing Age will support the champion and train the volunteers. The volunteers can visit residents individually, at a time that is convenient to both them and the care home, which means it's not dependent on a group of volunteers being available at the same time each week. More information can be found at www.embracingage.org.uk.

The key to success is building a good relationship with the care home. Most care homes would love to have trained volunteers to visit residents, but a few might be nervous. This is understandable, if they don't know you or the motivation behind volunteers visiting. It's important that they know you are not there with an inspector's hat on, or to criticise, but to be supportive to both residents and staff alike.

BUILDING A RELATIONSHIP WITH YOUR LOCAL CARE HOME

Extended lockdowns during the COVID-19 pandemic challenged us to develop creative ways of supporting care homes and building trust with staff. But you don't need a lockdown to implement any of the following ideas that will help you to build a trusting relationship with your local care home.

KINDNESS TO CARE STAFF GIFT BAGS

We don't need a pandemic to thank care home staff for all their hard work and dedication in looking after some of the oldest and frailest people in our community. Why not bless the staff at your local care home with a thank you gift bag of goodies? You could include hand cream, lip balm, chocolate, scented candles and handwritten thank you notes from members of your congregation. Take the opportunity to let them know that their local church is praying for them. Everyone loves to be shown appreciation.

CARDS OF KINDNESS

Handwritten letters and cards warm my heart and bring a smile to my face. I'm sure I'm not alone in that. Mobilise your church community to make and write cards to the residents of your local care home. Children can get involved by drawing pictures.

PLANTS AND FLOWERS

Plants and flowers are another way to bring joy. We have seen some lovely examples of this. A church supplied their local care home with plants for a sensory garden and another sent seeds for residents to plant and grow on their windowsills. On the Isle of Wight, a Bouquets of Blessing project was started, sending regular floral bouquets to local care homes.

Knitted aquariums

This is a fun way to get members of your church community engaged, and create a fabulous marine display that will put a smile on the faces of care home residents and staff.

Christmas gifts

Many care home residents do not have friends or family to give them Christmas gifts, so there's a lovely opportunity here for the Church to fill the void and create thoughtful gifts for residents.

It's worth checking with the care home first before implementing these ideas – it's no good going all out with a colourful knitted aquarium if the home has nowhere to put it! And we don't want to presume what the needs of the care home are – that isn't a good way of building trust.

Church services in care homes

Many churches run services in care homes on a regular basis, either monthly, fortnightly or weekly. These have a vital role in providing spiritual nourishment for residents. In some areas, churches have worked together to ensure that all care homes in their locality have a regular service. This book does not seek to be an A to Z guide of how to run a care home service, but will point you in the direction of good practice and useful resources.[5]

The move to online worship services during the pandemic has created new opportunities for church services in care homes. Whilst online can never replace in-person, if care home services are only happening monthly or fortnightly, it might be worth considering what online resources you could offer in between.

PARCHE

Parche have more than 23 years of experience in leading services in care homes. As a Christian charity based in Eastbourne, their initial vision was that every care home in the area would have a Christian team visiting at least once a month, to lead a half-hour worship service, befriend residents and where possible, pray for individuals. Now their vision is that every care home in the UK should have the same. They have developed training and resources to equip churches for this ministry,[6] and their founder, Buddy Reeve, tells some amazing stories of lives transformed:

A dear lady in her 90s, Ann, would not attend our services at first. When I started a Bible study she came and after several months said she was at last understanding the Scriptures. She then accepted a daily reading booklet and after a few weeks said she had prayed the prayer at the back to become a Christian. She now loves the services and is always asking when we will come again.

Another lady, Mary, had a serious stroke and I used to visit her in her room. I told her we had a Parche service in the lounge and she asked what it was about. When I explained she said, 'I'm not a Christian!'

I continued to visit her each month and met her husband who visited every day. After a few months she became weaker and one day when she was very poorly she said, 'How do I become a Christian?'

I explained simply about Jesus, the cross, and our need for forgiveness. She then prayed to ask Jesus to forgive her and be her Saviour. That was the last time I saw her as she died the next day. A short time later I met her husband and he said, 'The last thing Mary said to me was, "Frank, I'm a Christian now."'

The sequel is that two years later Frank was in hospital

and I visited. We talked about Mary and her decision to trust in Jesus. When I asked if he would like to do the same he said yes. So he too prayed for Jesus to forgive him and come into his life and be his Saviour. What a joy to know they are now both with the Lord in heaven.

Len was an atheist. He did not attend services, as for him science had all the answers. He was adamant, when I chatted to him, that he would never believe there was a God. However, he welcomed my visits and he knew all about Parche and was always gentle and gracious. One day he was in awful pain and I asked if I could pray and ask Jesus to take away his pain. He said, 'Do anything you want!' So I prayed and asked Jesus to heal him. The answer was immediate and remarkable. Len was completely healed and said, 'Oh, that's wonderful; He's here!' It was a very special moment and after a few minutes of silence in God's presence I asked Len if he wanted Jesus to be with him all the time. 'Yes I do,' he answered, so we prayed and Len received Him as Saviour. All his unbelief was swept away in a moment of time thanks to God's grace.

STORIES FOR THE SOUL

Stories for the Soul came out of the Godly Play initiative and supports the spiritual wellbeing of care home residents through community, Christian stories and creativity. Biblical stories are presented in a visual, tactile way that encourages engagement and gives opportunity to wonder on the meaning and respond in a creative way. Storytellers need to undergo the Godly Play training to use this approach. Our Church at Home is a more recent resource developed by Stories for the Soul during the pandemic, based around Christian festivals and biographies.[7]

OTHER RESOURCES

Embracing Age has gathered together online resources for teams running services in care homes, including links to Methodist Homes resources, Stories for the Soul and Parche.[8]

Often those running services in care homes see so much need, especially around loneliness and isolation, and do not know how to address it. This is where befriending residents can work hand in hand with regular services. Those running the service will already have built a trusting relationship with care home staff.

ANNA CHAPLAINCY

Aware of how rapidly the population is ageing, and with ordained clergy/ministers having limited time to visit people, Anglicans and Methodists signed a covenant in the Hampshire town of Alton in 2009 to collaborate more closely in various areas of ministry, one of which was supporting older people.

Anna Chaplaincy[9] developed from this first step, the title, Anna Chaplain, being chosen for its echoes of Anna, the widow and faithful older person who, together with Simeon, is described in St Luke's gospel as recognising the baby Jesus as the Messiah and the fulfilment of God's promises.

Debbie Thrower, the former broadcaster who is an Anglican licensed lay minister, was the first Anna Chaplain, developing the model before joining The Bible Reading Fellowship in 2014. The Anna Chaplaincy team is expanding the network with the charity's help right across the UK. As well as spreading to other parts of Hampshire, there are now Anna Chaplains on the South Coast, in Kent, West and East Sussex, the Midlands and the north-east.

Being community-based, an Anna Chaplain may spend time visiting people in residential care, or in their own private homes, or attending clubs and groups where people gather post-retirement.

The main purposes of an Anna Chaplain are to offer spiritual support to older people who are living in care homes and sheltered housing complexes, their relatives and staff who look after them. Alongside this they promote the spiritual welfare of older people in the wider community, particularly those facing challenges living independently.

In practice this involves helping older people reflect on their spiritual journey, including the healing of memories and dealing with outstanding issues; offering spiritual support so that older people may live more peacefully in their last years and prepare to face the end of their earthly lives and acting as an advocate for the needs of older people in church and in the wider community.

Anna Chaplains come alongside relatives and staff working with older people by helping them to better understand the spiritual issues that older people face in the latter stages of their lives. They also support relatives with the responsibilities of caring for older people in their family and offer spiritual support to staff dealing with the sometimes distressing circumstances that they encounter when working with older people in their care.

Anna Chaplains are also involved with churches, helping to inform and coordinate the work amongst older people, to enable them to value their contribution in the life of the church, as well as to understand the particular needs older people may have, and to consider what constitutes 'successful ageing' and so prepare for more positive experiences in older age.

A growing number of volunteers, called Anna Friends, work alongside the Anna Chaplains, often giving a few hours a week to suit their own circumstances and play to their strengths and gifts.

Each Anna Chaplain is appointed and authorised by, and sent out under the authority of, their church or local group of Churches Together. An Anna Chaplain never operates under their own auspices, because of the fundamental need for accountability.

Any church considering setting up Anna Chaplaincy should talk to the Anna Chaplaincy team at The Bible Reading Fellowship and get advice.[10] They have a well-worn route guiding churches and individuals through the process of either setting up a chaplaincy or discerning a vocation to this form of ministry. Anna Chaplaincy is a registered trademark and cannot be used without a licence.

Debbie Thrower shares this story:

Anna Chaplains meet a lot of people living alone. Even a resident in a care home, surrounded by people, may feel painfully isolated. A person may beat themselves up for being alone; blaming themselves that they now spend long periods on their own, the inference being, 'It must be because I am unlovable.'

As we get older, we all have a tendency to rake over the past, perhaps to make sense of it. One person who remains much in mind is someone we'll call Maurice. He lived alone, latterly seeing only one or two people a week when walking became difficult and he was more and more confined to his home.

A younger friend of the family did his shopping, but otherwise he had few contemporaries left with whom to share memories of the past or to converse with about his hobbies. He had worked in agriculture, and been quite closely associated with the church as a boy, singing in a choir. He loved music. But the painful death of a family member had made it hard for Maurice to trust that God was 'really there' or to have confidence in 'a benign Creator'.

When he had been more mobile, he made a point of attending coffee mornings and other church social events. But the last two years or so of his life he experienced intense loneliness, and doubts about what might lie beyond death. He had a fear of dying; he would speak about the physical aspects of death and funerals. It became something of a preoccupation.

I think the visits from an Anna Chaplain made a very significant difference to the quality of his life in those closing years and final weeks. Firstly, the chaplain accompanied him to find a new pet, after the death of his last one. This was a key aspect of his life and was a source of interest and companionship, as human company became more problematic because of mobility issues.

She was able to answer his fears about dying and begin to explore with him the basis for Christian hope of life after death. She gave him the opportunity to speak about the loss of people he had loved dearly and about the circumstances of their deaths which still evidently troubled him.

Lastly, she was someone with whom he could laugh, tell stories, discuss current events and she could bring him local news of the outside world – and copies of the church magazines. He was hungry for snippets of news about the people, the familiar faces from his town he was no longer seeing for himself.

He faced his last few weeks of life with greater fortitude than might otherwise have been possible. He had known friendship from someone whom he knew would not forsake him when he needed human company the most.

Maurice, as it turned out, died in his sleep (one hopes) peacefully. The Anna Chaplain who had visited him regularly then conducted his funeral. She was able to reflect that though he wasn't a regular churchgoer in his adult life, he had respect and admiration for the Christians with whom he had come into contact. One day he'd exclaimed, 'My, how those Methodists love one another. They're some of the kindest people I've ever known.'

Maurice had known God's love through the kindness of his

church community who became his friends, and in particular the Anna Chaplain, one of the select few to whom he would send a Christmas card.

Maurice's pet, by the way, was successfully rehomed.

INTERGENERATIONAL ACTIVITIES IN CARE HOMES

A simple way a church could engage in intergenerational care home activities is to encourage the mother and toddler group to meet at the care home on a regular basis.

When thinking of intergenerational ideas that include care home residents, it's tempting to get into a 'do for' mode, rather than 'doing together'. For example, in a meeting recently we were discussing how we could promote connections between the generations at a care home where our church runs fortnightly services. Two ideas we had were, firstly, to get the youth group to create little gifts (e.g. lavender bags) for the residents, and write a card to go with them. The young people would then visit the care home, give out the gifts and spend time chatting with residents. Secondly, to get the children's group to visit at Easter and Christmas and sing to the residents. These are both lovely ideas, but notice that in each case the residents are passive recipients, other than when chatting with the young people. Ideally, when planning intergenerational activity, we should be trying to engage both young and old as active participants. So, in the first case, the young people could still write a card, introducing themselves and inviting the residents to a craft morning at the home, where together with the young people they will make lavender bags, or do another activity. In the second scenario, the children could be taught songs that will be familiar to the older people, so that both young and old can sing together. Of course, with all these ideas it's important to get the permission from care home staff.

There are many online resources to inspire ideas for intergenerational activity and we have put some of them together on our website.[11]

Recently I helped set up an intergenerational gardening project at a local care home, facilitated by an outdoor learning organisation. A group of children from a primary school did gardening and nature crafts with residents, to bring the benefits of being outdoors along with intergenerational connections. Perhaps not surprisingly, both the residents and the children had a wonderful time, and it was interesting to learn that most of the residents showed improvements in their physical abilities in at least one area that was measured as part of the project. There's no reason why this sort of initiative couldn't be set up between a church and a care home if there are keen gardeners in your congregation.

TRUTH BE TOLD

Truth Be Told[12] is an intergenerational storytelling group, rooted in Christian truth, involving parents, toddlers and care home residents, led by a trained facilitator, or storyteller. Each week a short tale of hope is put at the centre of some songs, along with a treasure trove of props and a multitude of imaginative interactions. Truth Be Told mobilises the 'parent' generation who are motivated to attend stimulating activities with their children and offer them rounded experiences of life. Part of the storyteller's role is to create a sense of community among the parents (who need intergenerational relationships too) and bring it into the care home. Truth Be Told engages residents by using music from the past, and making space for reminiscence, as well as playing with the imagination of everyone to evoke memories and create new, positive and reassuring experiences.

Gemma Gillard, the founder of Truth Be Told tells these stories:

Pat is a care home resident living with dementia. She was quite unsettled and agitated before the second session of Truth Be Told. She said that she didn't know what she should be doing but as soon as the children arrived, her demeanour changed. Week by week Pat became increasingly involved and relaxed. She was able to articulate the effects of her dementia to parents in a way that helped them understand how she was experiencing the session and so that they were able to respond to her needs and sensitively encourage her to participate. By the final week, Pat was clearly enjoying herself so much that she got up to dance with one of the mums. She even helped to wave the parachute over the children and played with balloons.

If you happened to walk past Mary, she would tickle you wherever she could. Everyone would laugh and make light of it. And Mary would whoop with laughter too. But after every session the storyteller would reflect to themselves: if 20 years ago, Mary could look ahead and see herself now, she would be mortified. A caricature of her real self, totally uninhibited and manic, this version of Mary was quite intimidating. The children had become adept at avoiding her tickles, some giggling, some retreating shyly, until one morning. As the children entered the room, Mary automatically opened her arms for one of them to run into and astonishingly, one did! Lottie clearly shared Mary's visceral instinct for a hug and they embraced. No tickles. No whoops. As Lottie snuggled into Mary's lap, Mary stroked her back and was clothed with dignity. Her role was restored and a beautiful relationship was kindled.

PUPPET MINISTRY IN CARE HOMES

Puppet ministry is more usually associated with holiday clubs, school assemblies and family church services, but Puppet Power, based in Grimsby, have been taking puppets into care homes for nearly 20 years, and describe it as 'one of the most surprising journeys the team has experienced'. They go into about 20 different care homes over the course of a year, and perform a mixture of popular parody songs with a Christian message, Bible stories and other well-known songs and hymns. The parody songs include 'Witness All Over the World' ('Rocking All Over the World' by Status Quo), 'Baa Baa We're Lambs' ('Barbara-Ann', by the Regents, popularised by the Beach Boys), and 'I Will Always Love You' (Whitney Houston). Each performance lasts between 30 and 50 minutes.

Residents are happy to join in with the singing and interact with the puppets. Unlike normal puppet shows, the puppets are taken outside of the puppet theatre for part of the session, so that the residents can meet the characters, interact with them, touch and feel them. This is particularly helpful for residents with limited sight and hearing.

Ian Jones is the director of Puppet Power and the managing director of One Way UK Creative Ministries (www.onewayuk. com), where they design and build many of the puppets for teams all over the world. He explains:

The variety and colour of the puppets used, with the choreography and movement, and in particular the familiar music, help bring back memories and it is wonderful to see residents so animated and hear them singing along, remembering all the words to the songs. It is fantastic to see the response of the audience, which is made up not only of the residents, but also their family, grandchildren, visitors and not forgetting the staff too!

The residents now are from the era and time when many of them would have gone to Sunday School and attended church on a regular basis. They know the nativity story, and can remember many Bible stories with just a little prompting. This may change in time, but for now it is a joy to share the Gospel message with them, bringing back many happy memories and helping them to experience church in a different but familiar way again.

When care homes get in touch about booking a puppet show, Ian always lets them know it is a church puppet team and that their presentation has a Christian message, and this has never been an issue.

Reflecting on the challenges of using puppet ministry in care homes, Ian writes:

One of the real challenges when going into care homes is the amount of space you have. We have been squashed in a bay window, a fireplace and often in front of the TV! Any more than four or five people and you may not have space to move. Occasionally you may have a small audience, with some residents asleep or possibly even abusive. The key thing is to keep going, try to not let it affect you, and be assured that the staff will know the best way to deal with each resident and calm anyone down. Similarly, because of the security getting into and out of care homes, along with the space limitations, careful packing of the puppets and equipment is necessary so that you have what you need but are not bringing anything extra. We don't charge the care homes for our visits but we ask where possible if they can make a donation to our ministry needs – the ongoing expense of buying new puppets and equipment. For bookings which are not local to us, I would ask for travel expenses at cost.

Each care home is different. Some are much better at

getting the residents involved, sometimes providing basic musical instruments for the residents to use. It is so helpful when staff stay with the residents to encourage them to join in, to stop them moving around or becoming disruptive. Encourage the residents to participate and don't be afraid to let them interact with you and the puppets! This can often result in them sharing their stories – one lady told us that she particularly liked how the puppets all moved around, as it reminded her of when she was a dancer in the West End theatres! Normally we would not take the puppets out of the stage, but at care homes it does work and residents really do like to meet the characters and have their photo taken with them. Again, it is particularly important where residents have poor sight, for them to be able to touch and feel the puppets' fabric, fur and shape.

Ian is a strong advocate of using puppets in care homes. He concludes:

It is a wonderful ministry to be a part of, with a unique set of challenges but also incredible opportunities too. We have many calls/texts from the homes on how the residents enjoyed our visit or were touched by the message we gave. People who are always pacing around sit still to watch us, even someone who had not spoken since arriving at the home, started talking to the puppets and joined in singing the songs. I pray that as you go into care homes, you will be greatly blessed as you bless the residents, their families and the staff, and never stop learning! You too can experience the joy and transforming impact puppetry can have – it can be massive!

CHAPTER 6

ACTIVITIES IN CHURCH BUILDINGS

M any churches are blessed with accessible space at the heart of their community that is ideal for hosting activities for seniors. We'll spend this chapter exploring ideas that can be facilitated in accessible church buildings. But if you are part of a church that does not have your own building, or a church whose facilities are not accessible, in the following chapter we'll highlight other ways you can establish a ministry amongst seniors.

WHAT MAKES A CHURCH BUILDING ACCESSIBLE?

Accessibility of church buildings is a huge subject and not limited to the needs of older people. Under the Equality Act of 2010, churches must take reasonable steps to ensure their buildings and activities are accessible to everyone. There may be challenges involved in making historic buildings and those in conservation areas more accessible, especially when planning and other permissions are needed. There are helpful websites covering church accessibility in detail,[1] so I just want to pick up on a few considerations, some more obvious than others. Clearly, if your church has steps up to the entrance with no other means of access, then this may be a problem to those whose mobility is limited. Ease of access also needs to be considered for the toilet facilities.

But even before someone enters your building there are things to consider. Do you have a specified disabled parking space; in fact, does your church have any parking spaces at all? My church is on a busy main road, with very limited parking within the church grounds and parking restrictions in all the surrounding roads. However, we do have a bus stop immediately outside, with buses arriving every few minutes from five different routes, although not all older people with mobility issues will be able or confident to use public transport.

Then consider the journey from the outer perimeter of your church up to the building's entrance. Is the path smooth and step-free? And is the entrance obvious? I have visited several churches to attend midweek activities for seniors. One of the first things that often confuses me is which door I should use. Some churches have so many entrances. It may be obvious on a Sunday morning when the church is busier, or to those who attend regularly, which entrance to use, but to a newcomer, church buildings can seem quite intimidating and confusing. There may be life and bustle inside the church hall, but from the outside it can seem quiet, leaving people wondering if they have come to the correct venue or entrance. Consider creating large and obvious signage.

Seating is also an important consideration. Sofas may look cosy and homely, but low chairs can be a challenge for people with reduced mobility to get up from. Comfortably cushioned chairs with a higher seat are much better and it's worth having a few with arms for those who need the extra leverage to stand up. You may want to consider having seat coverings that can be wiped clean, for people who are struggling with incontinence.

HEARING LOSS AND VISUAL IMPAIRMENT

If you are going to run an activity that involves speaking to a group, it is worth considering amplification and a hearing loop, for those who are deaf. Also consider the needs of those with visual impairment by having large print available on any written communication. Those with sight loss may appreciate being invited to join in conversations if they are standing alone and should also be asked about what further assistance they would find helpful. Torch Trust have produced an informative website on how churches can become sight-loss friendly.[2]

DEMENTIA INCLUSIVE CHURCHES

If you have jumped straight to this chapter, I encourage you to backtrack and read the section on dementia, which provides a comprehensive introduction to the subject. When thinking about developing a dementia friendly church, it's important to understand that it starts with dementia friendly people. After all, the church is the *ekklesia*, 'the called out ones' – the people rather than the building. You can have all the physical adjustments and adaptations to create a dementia friendly building, but without dementia friendly people it's all rather meaningless. A simple first step, therefore, in becoming dementia inclusive is to organise a short dementia awareness talk for members of your congregation. Often there are local organisations and people willing to facilitate these sessions, such as Dementia Friends.[3]

We want to create an environment where people living with dementia and their loved ones feel welcome, included and able to participate. There are numerous online resources about becoming a dementia inclusive church,[4] which cover both the people and the building. Livability have produced a helpful guide that can be freely downloaded from their website.[5]

Small, inexpensive adaptations can be made to the environment to help people living with dementia, such as clear signage at eye level, with good contrast, particularly at toilets and exits, and contrasting sanitary ware, enabling the toilet to be seen more clearly. Some changes may be prohibitively expensive, like replacing flooring, but an awareness of perception problems that someone with dementia may experience can help to reassure them if they become troubled. A dark mat may appear to be a hole, so that the person thinks they will fall if they step forward. A shiny floor can appear wet and slippery. It can also be helpful to have a quiet space available for people to retreat if they are experiencing sensory overload or an emotional meltdown, and volunteers available to give discreet, personalised support to individuals.

Ensuring that our buildings are accessible is the first step in creating a sense of welcome, but there are other small things that can be done to help people feel at ease.

CREATING A FRIENDLY WELCOME

As well as large and obvious signage to point people to the correct entrance, an even friendlier welcome is created by having greeters stationed at strategic places outside, to provide a reassuring smile and point people in the right direction. The impact of this was brought home to me when I attended a conference at a church in Claygate that runs a large Connections programme for its seniors. I was slightly apprehensive as I parked my car, since I was attending on my own, but the sense of welcome I felt from the team members who were standing outside, greeting people and giving directions, made me feel at ease and as if they were genuinely pleased to see me.

A tip I would highly recommend is to use name labels for all the guests and helpers every week. I don't know about you, but I am rubbish at remembering names and once you've been introduced to someone it can then be very awkward to ask their name again the following hour, week or month. In my experience, whenever I have introduced sticky name labels, even to established groups, everyone has appreciated them. I always jokingly say that it's because I'm so terrible at remembering names, and very often people will confess that they are too. It also ensures that if a new guest arrives at an established group they don't feel so much like an outsider or have the pressure of remembering everyone's name.

Make sure your volunteers are prepped in the vital importance of a warm welcome, whatever their other roles may be, and to be mindful of people looking uncomfortable or ill at ease, with ideas of how to draw them into conversations or activities with others.

Accessibility and welcome are fundamental to any activity you undertake in your church building, and there is a myriad to choose from. In previous chapters we explored ideas to support people living with dementia, and their carers. The following section looks at other activities for seniors that can be facilitated in a church building.

Exercise classes

Keeping fit is an important aspect of remaining healthy as we age, so an exercise class geared towards seniors can be popular. This could be anything from Zumba Gold, to Pilates or chair-based exercise. You will need to find and pay a trained instructor to run the group, so may consider charging a small amount to cover costs. It's a good idea to provide refreshments at the end of the class to encourage people to stay and socialise.

CHAIROBICS

A retired physiotherapist in her 80s started an exercise class for seniors about 20 years ago at her church in West London. She had a heart for both exercise and outreach, and saw the group as an opportunity to keep people active and healthy, reduce the risk of falls and reduce isolation, as well as welcoming people across the threshold of the church into a worshipping community. She ran the group well into her 90s, when it was taken over by another physiotherapist in the church. The session consists of 40 minutes of exercise and 20 minutes of tea and biscuits, and is attended by a mix of church members and others in the local community. The numbers have fluctuated over the years, depending on who was leading, but currently has about 20 regulars. In the early days, when it was run by church members, the class was free, but in more recent years the church has needed to look outside the congregation for a suitably qualified physiotherapist, and charges £2 per session to cover the costs.

The seniors' pastor at St Stephen's gives the following advice for those considering starting an exercise class:

1. Be clear about the vision and purpose of the group and make sure an influential person in the group, whether the instructor or a regular attendee, gets the vision for the outreach aspect and can carry it.
2. Include a social time at the end, as there are not many opportunities to chat while you are exercising, meaning it can be difficult to build relationship.
3. A good-quality instructor is essential – attendees need to feel that the exercise is safe and that it is working.
4. Set it up prayerfully.

COMPUTER CLASSES

Many older people can feel left behind in this technological age. Even those with some computer skills can feel nervous about viruses and scams. Consider a regular club where participants can develop their technology skills in an unrushed environment where they feel able to ask 'silly' questions. Some participants will be able to bring their laptop or tablet, but it can be useful to have spare computers available for those who are new to technology.

About eight years ago, when I worked for a local Age UK, I was approached by a Baptist church wanting to reach out to older people in their community. They were a small congregation with a big heart, but short on manpower. They partnered with us to run a weekly Zumba Gold exercise class and a computer club. We provided the resources for the computer club, including laptops and a teacher to run a six-week beginners' course. The church provided the hall, refreshments and two people to welcome participants and give individual support. Participants paid a small amount for the six-week course, to cover some of the costs for the teacher. At the end of the course the learners were enjoying it so much that they wanted to continue to meet. The club continued, without the teacher but with volunteers from the church, new people were added and it became a wonderful, supportive community. At the local Age UK we had a volunteer driver who would deliver the laptops to the various computer clubs and courses that we were involved with, and he always loved going to the one at this church, saying of all the clubs it was the most friendly and there was a real sense of community. I recently bumped into members of the church involved in the computer club and it is still thriving. They have between 12 to 16 people attending weekly, and have more volunteers to help, provided by the local Age UK. It has continued to be a very sociable community with people spending as much time chatting as they do working on their IT skills.

Clearly there are some set-up costs to consider, such as providing laptops or tablets, and you may not have the resources or experience to run a beginners' course. But there may be local organisations you can partner with, or others in your congregation with the relevant experience and confidence to run a course. You can also add special sessions about online scams and viruses, which your local police may be willing to present, or run workshops on tablets or mobile phones, where participants bring their own.

KNIT AND NATTER, ART OR CRAFT GROUPS

If you have people in your congregation with a passion for creativity and craft, they may love the opportunity to share this with others. In a knit and natter group, participants bring whatever knitting or crochet project they are in the process of creating and simply work on it in the company of others, developing new friendships and old as they knit. Novices can pick the brains of those more experienced if they are stuck on a certain section of their pattern. The group facilitator provides a comfortable environment and refreshments. These can be great places for intergenerational connections, enabling experienced knitters to pass on their skills to others.

Art and craft groups take rather more organisation, creativity and planning, as the facilitators often plan different projects to complete, resourcing the necessary materials.

CRAFTY CUPPA

Crafty Cuppa is a fortnightly craft club for seniors pioneered by the minister of Hampton Wick Baptist Church, who wanted to encourage creative members of her congregation, mostly older, to share their skills with others, in an environment that encouraged community and addressed social isolation and loneliness. She also wanted to create a stepping stone into the church family, especially for older folk who had once had a faith but then lost it. Crafty Cuppa leads on to Good Companions, a monthly lunch followed by a short service geared towards seniors, and then hopefully encourages them into the full body of the church.

The two-hour session starts with a craft activity, followed by a break for tea and homemade cake. Some people bring craft work with them to do whilst chatting, and are happy to share their skills, while others just come for a chat. There is also a board game available for those who don't want to participate in the craft.

The biggest challenge they have found is making the group known in the local community. They produced a flier and circulated it in the area to places like the local doctor's surgery, the community hall and other organisations working with older people, but few have come through this. Nonetheless, it has been a joy to see the seniors sharing their creative skills with others, and making contact with people who would otherwise not come into the church.

The minister at Hampton Wick Baptist Church gives this advice to those considering starting a regular craft session for seniors:

1. Make sure you have a warm and comfortable place to meet – it could be a home.
2. Be willing to adapt to the personnel who come. Don't set an agenda! If they want to silently knit, if they want to chat nonstop, if they want to do something other than craft, like play a game – then let it happen. What's important is the needs of those who come.

3. Make homemade cakes if possible. People living on their own tend not to do that for themselves.
4. Remember special occasions – birthdays, hospital visits, etc.
5. Pray! I may have put this last but it is fundamental to the success of it all. Ultimately we are seeking to make disciples and God will use something very simple like a 'crafternoon' if we see it as outreach in its simplest form and not just a cosy afternoon of chat and craft.

SENIORS' LIFE GROUP OR BIBLE STUDY

Life groups are the heartbeat of many churches, enabling relationships to grow and deepen in a way that there is not space for at a Sunday service. However, many groups meet on midweek evenings in the homes of church members, which may present a problem for older adults who do not like to be out late, or for those with reduced mobility, where accessibility may be an issue. A daytime midweek group that meets at the church building can provide an alternative. It can also be opened to others who find attending evening groups a challenge, so that different generations are enabled to connect.

Life groups provide an opportunity to study the Bible together, apply it to our lives, share openly and pray for one another. Billy Graham once said, 'All my life I've been taught how to die, but no-one ever taught me how to grow old.' And John Stott echoed the same sentiment: 'I knew I had to prepare for eternity, but no-one told me I had to prepare for being old'. In a life group for seniors, time can be spent focusing on some of the challenges and joys of ageing from a biblical perspective.

God's word is relevant at every stage of our lives. I love the Narnia Chronicles by C. S. Lewis. In *Prince Caspian* Lucy sees Aslan again and they have a profound exchange:

'Aslan, Aslan. Dear Aslan,' sobbed Lucy. 'At last.'

The great beast rolled over on his side so that Lucy fell, half sitting and half lying between his front paws. He bent forward and just touched her nose with his tongue. His warm breath came all round her. She gazed up into the large wise face.

'Welcome, child,' he said.

'Aslan,' said Lucy, 'you're bigger.'

'That is because you are older, little one,' answered he.

'Not because you are?'

'I am not. But every year you grow, you will find me bigger.'

Every year we grow we will find God bigger: there is always more. As we get older, He gets bigger! That has certainly been my experience. There are new riches to discover in His word and apply to our lives, greater understanding of the mystery of faith. At a seniors' life group recently, we were talking about persistent prayer – this is as relevant to a 25-year-old as it is to someone who is 85. We don't always have to look for truths that are relevant to ageing when leading a Bible study with seniors. As Paul tells us, all of the Bible is 'God-breathed and is useful for teaching, rebuking, correcting and training in righteousness'.[6]

That's not to say that we should never focus on issues relating to ageing. There is a place for this, and a number of resources have been produced to help facilitate discussion.

The Omega Course developed by St Paul's Church in Kingston[7] is a six-week study that gives participants the opportunity to explore and discuss the challenges and blessings of ageing from a biblical perspective. When the group was facilitated amongst an established group of seniors who had already built a level of safety, they found that people were very open to sharing their thoughts and offer words of wisdom to one another. Participants were very positive about the course and felt it gave them lots to reflect on and think about.

In 2019 the Salvation Army produced a discipleship resource for small groups of seniors, with 30 conversation starters covering seven themes including growing old gracefully, identity, trust and forgiveness. Each conversation includes activities, discussions, teaching, reflections and prayers, so that little preparation is required by the group leader.[8]

FOOD GLORIOUS FOOD

Eating together can be highly sociable so it's not surprising that lots of activities revolve around food, from the simplicity of a coffee morning or afternoon tea with delicious homemade cakes, to more involved lunch clubs. A word of caution about lunch clubs: they are labour intensive and sometimes kept going by ageing helpers who would benefit from hanging up their apron and enjoying being served instead. That's not to put an age limit on helpers, or to discriminate against age, as we shall see in the examples that follow. I know of a wonderful lady in her 80s who sees it as her ministry to help with washing up, and I've seen her do this for a huge Christmas lunch that fed about 70 people. She was practically the last woman standing when the rest of us younger ones were flagging! But sometimes faithful ageing servants need permission to step out of their roles, if and when it becomes a burden to them, and not have to soldier on because it seems like no one else will fill their shoes.

If all your manpower and resources are going into keeping a historic lunch club alive, you might want to look at other options. This could be getting caterers to prepare the food, providing a simpler meal, such as soup, or moving location to a community café or local restaurant where people can order and pay for their own meals. You may be able to negotiate a discount. Of course you would need to check on the accessibility of both the restaurant and the toilet facilities.

Despite the time and resources that go into lunch clubs, they can be a huge blessing, providing a nutritious meal and opportunities for social interactions. I recently heard a story about an older lady who had lived alone on a council estate for many years. She came regularly to the lunch club at the local church because she said it was the only place she felt loved.

LUNCH CLUB AT TWICKENHAM GREEN BAPTIST CHURCH

Twickenham Green Baptist Church is a growing congregation in West London. Their lunch club started as weekly light lunches for mums and children during the summer holidays of 1987. When autumn term began, the volunteers decided to continue with more substantial hot meals during the winter months to help the homeless and lonely – anyone was welcome.

At first only about half a dozen people from the church came, but as word spread the numbers grew, mainly older people who lived locally. It has continued every Thursday, with breaks during the school holidays, and numbers have fluctuated between 15 and 35 people. A three-course meal is served, for which guests make a small contribution.

The highlights for the team have been building friendships and listening to and sharing in the lives of others. Christmas lunches have been particularly memorable, with school children singing carols and Santa visiting. One Christmas, the children gathered around the piano and spontaneously started singing along as their pianist, Jack, himself a senior citizen, played. It was totally unplanned, and quite wonderful. They have also celebrated many birthdays, including special 80s and 90s.

One helper, who is a carer for her spouse, found being

involved in the lunch club was a lifeline, and gave her time to just be herself. Another lady who moved away from the area still came by taxi because she had made such meaningful friendships. They have found that quite a few lunch club participants enjoy coming to other church events.

There have also been challenges. As a small team of just two or three regular volunteers, it has required a lot of commitment. They never know for sure how many people will come, or the amount of food needed, but God has always provided and they have never turned anyone away hungry. Sometimes due to sickness or family responsibilities, they have been short staffed but have been blessed and amazed at how people have offered to help. Several participants have gone from being served to serving or washing up.

Their advice to anyone considering starting a lunch club is to keep it simple to start with. Ensure you have two or three people who are really behind you, and can share responsibility for all the various jobs, such as shopping, preparation, cooking and cleaning. It's also a good idea to have a few standby volunteers for unexpected absences. Of course, volunteers will need to be trained to comply with Food Hygiene Standards.

St Stephen's Monday lunch club

This was set up by a faithful couple called Joy and Alfred in the 1970s, in response to a report about the loneliness and isolation experienced by older people. St Stephen's is a large church, and as the lunch club expanded they were able to put together two teams, each with their own head cook, along with a network of other bakers and cooking volunteers. The lunch club runs fortnightly so that each team is only on duty once a month. Joy and Alfred ran the lunch club well into their 90s, with Joy as the head cook for her team. They saw those who came to lunch club as their flock and would visit people who were sick, as well as bringing flowers from their garden for the tables, to go on the beautifully laundered white cotton tablecloths.

About 40 to 45 people attend the lunch club every fortnight, and pay a small amount for a cooked lunch followed by a speaker or live music.

One of the biggest challenges has been managing the occasional guest who does not have good social skills, which can affect the welcome that other guests receive, especially those who are new. Placing a host helper at the table concerned can help, but it does require having a volunteer available to do this, who has the necessary skills to manage the situation. Also, some guests like to sit in the same place every week, so that there is not always space for a host volunteer.

There have been some wonderful highlights too. One gentleman was brought to the lunch club by the community occupational therapist. His wife had recently died and he was becoming increasingly depressed and isolated. As he walked up the path towards the church he bumped into a lady who had been a friend of his wife. This encouraged him to stay and keep attending, and he turned out to be quite a gatherer of people, as he invited others to come, and his table would often be filled with lively chatter and raucous laughter.

CONNECTIONS

Holy Trinity Claygate has developed a wonderful initiative for welcoming older people and enabling them to socialise and build friendships. Aptly named Connections, it aims to connect people to God and with each other, with the emphasis very much on relationships.

Before their fortnightly Tuesday gatherings, volunteers set up the church café-style to prepare for more than 100 guests who regularly come along and are offered a warm welcome with hot drinks and homemade cakes. Flowers are put on the tables, and guests are invited to participate in a host of other optional activities, including craft, mini hand massages, gentle exercises, jigsaws, shared hobbies and special interest tables, which allow guests to chat whilst participating together.

The team of volunteers place great emphasis on ensuring that guests feel welcomed and at ease. The church aims to help guests experience the love of God through the friendships they build at Connections, and the loving care they find there. During the morning, there's a light touch 'thought for the day' shared by one of the leaders and there are always volunteers for guests to talk to and pray with.

Connections sees a large number of men attending, which is unusual for many seniors' groups. This is partly due to the male volunteers who are particularly good at coming alongside the older gentlemen, but also many of the activities aim to appeal to men, particularly the special interest tables.

As Connections grew in popularity, the church organised a Connections Coffee Stop meeting on alternate Tuesdays to the main Connections gathering. This is another opportunity for seniors to socialise over coffee and biscuits, without the extra activities available at the Connections group.

Connections has been running for ten years at Holy Trinity and is part of their wider strategy to enable seniors to experience the love of God and move forward in their faith. They have recently started a separate Walk and Talk group for actively retired people, as they were aware that their Connections guests have been getting older over the decade and younger seniors are looking for something different, even though some are happy to come as helpers.

They also realised that they needed to be more intentional

about taking older people on in their faith journey, and have developed an innovative series called Hymns We Love, but more about that later.

A further recent development has been Pop up Connections, taking Connections into a care home so that those unable to get to the church don't miss out. Lovely flowers and homemade cakes enable them to provide a similar set-up in the care home environment and build relationships with residents.

Pippa Cramer, who developed Connections and heads up the ministry amongst seniors at Holy Trinity Claygate, emphasises the importance of prayer. Connections was set up prayerfully, and prayer saturates every aspect of their ministry and strategy.

MARY'S STORY

Mary is 99 years old. She had a spinal injury some years ago and is now confined to a wheelchair. She lives in a care home, close to Holy Trinity Claygate, where Connections is based, and her two daughters have been bringing her along for about nine years. For nearly all her life Mary has described herself as an agnostic, since she was unsure of what she really believed.

Pippa describes a visit she made to Mary in December 2017, in her care home:

Mary had been talking to her daughters about the end of her life, how she might like her funeral to be when the time came, and how she now thought she would like this to be in Holy Trinity Church. We had the most wonderful conversation. Mary told me that, surprisingly, she had found herself 'chatting' to God! Was this praying, she wondered? I assured her that this most certainly was! Praying is very simply chatting to God. She had never really spoken to Him before, and she found this so very comforting – being able to talk to God about things she was worried about, the future, day-to-day things. It was so precious to hear Mary speak about this. We moved on to talking about Christmas. How wonderful it was for Mary to think about the Christmas story now, and we talked about how God loved her so very much He sent His Son, Jesus, to this earth, to be born in a stable, to live as a man, and to then die on a cross so that she could have this wonderful relationship with God. It was as if a light had been switched on for Mary. I asked her if I could pray for her that afternoon. As I started to pray with her, she confidently joined in and 'chatted to God' herself! It was truly beautiful. As I drove away that day, I wept as I thought about God, how amazingly gracious and compassionate He is, that He would gently draw this darling lady to Himself after 95 years or so.

Both Mary and her daughters say that it has been going to Connections week by week, and the love and care that she has received over the years there, the warm welcome, the generosity – this has been what has impacted her faith and her belief now in Jesus. She feels that she has experienced God's love through the relationships she has formed at Connections. Her faith has recently become stronger through attending Hymns We Love at Holy Trinity, a gentle evangelistic series written for older people, helping them to explore the Christian faith using wonderful, well-loved hymns.

Pippa reflects, 'It has been such an amazing privilege to walk alongside Mary over these last few years. We continue to love and support her.'

CONNECTIONS AT ST JAMES HAMPTON HILL

Inspired by Connections in Claygate, members of St James's Church in Hampton Hill, an Anglican church with a congregation of about 100, decided to create their own Connections group. It was initiated by church member, Coryn, whose elderly and fragile mum was finding it hard to visit her circle of friends or have any social interaction following the death of her husband; she really only felt comfortable in her own surroundings. Coryn's mum was a lifelong member of St James's Church and was prepared to try attending a group activity in familiar surroundings. Sadly, she ultimately only managed a couple of sessions before her needs increased and she moved to a care home.

St James's Connections meets on the first Tuesday of each month, to coincide with the weekly communion service, which occurs immediately beforehand, and now also has an informal coffee time after the service on the second Tuesday of each month. Over the last 18 months they have developed their own format, which always includes:

- Fairtrade coffee or tea and homemade cakes.
- Table top games, which are always popular, such as Scrabble, Uno and cards, set out in a quieter area.
- A book and magazine swap (leftovers are taken to the local charity shop).
- A 500-piece jigsaw, which is surprisingly popular and always has participants, and encourages ongoing involvement as the jigsaw is stored until completed.
- A boxed jigsaw swap area has also developed.

Other regular activities include:

- Carpet bowls.
- A craft activity which Coryn usually chooses, as she enjoys craft, but this takes a bit more persuasion to get people to have a go!
- Occasional talks from members about interesting subjects, such as looking at local historical photos.
- A hearing clinic, run by an NHS volunteer, which is becoming popular as word has spread about it.
- A knitting circle with patterns, wool and needles provided – recently started and growing in popularity.

The number of people attending is variable, but usually averages about 15 to 20. Coryn is keen for it not to be perceived as a club for the elderly and lonely, but rather as a warm and welcoming event for anybody locally with a need or who just wants to share time with others. They have seen new friendships being developed.

To others who may want to start a Connection- type group, Coryn gives this advice:

- Be prepared to adapt your expectations. It will take time to grow.
- Develop slowly and take time to trial new ideas.
- Follow your instincts!

HOLIDAY AT HOME

Many activities close down over the summer months. Long days, combined with many families going on holiday, can increase the loneliness experienced by older people. Holiday at Home takes the idea of children's holiday clubs, and adapts it for seniors, enabling them to enjoy a week of companionship and other activities. This could include outings, crafts, hobbies, exercise, games and a 'thought for the day'. This popular idea usually happens on two to five consecutive days, but can be run as a weekly activity.

A church in South London that has hosted Holiday at Home for many years, changed it from an event over three to four days, to a weekly session on four consecutive Thursdays. The regular attendees were somewhat disgruntled by this change in routine, but by the end of the final session one of the oldest ladies got up and humbly admitted that despite being against the change, she had come to appreciate having something to look forward to each week. However, a weekly session does bring other logistical challenges, such as having to set up and down each week, rather than leaving everything in place.

A training booklet on running Holiday at Home, written by Liz Stacey from Winchester Baptist Church is available to freely download.[9]

TO PAY OR NOT TO PAY?

Whatever activity you decide to set up as a church, at some stage you will be faced with the question of whether to charge, or to offer it for free. There are no rights and wrongs about this. If you are a large, well-resourced church that wants to bless your community and can afford to cover the costs, you may decide to offer the activity free of charge. But if you are a smaller church with fewer resources that also wants to bless your community, but know that without a contribution from participants an activity will not be sustainable, you may decide to either charge a set amount or to invite contributions. Personally, I think charging a set amount is preferable, since everyone knows where they stand, and discretion can always be applied if you are aware of someone in financial difficulty.

For activities with higher set-up costs, such as computer

clubs, it's worth looking at local grant-givers to see if there are funds available. A memory café run by a Methodist church in my area participated in a local supermarket token scheme and was able to buy a range of specialised dementia activity resources.

Most of the activities mentioned in this chapter require the use of a church building. In the next chapter we'll explore ideas for churches that do not have a suitable building.

CHAPTER 7

No Building, No Problem

I have been part of a number of churches over the last 40 years that either did not have a church building (we met in a school), or the building had very poor accessibility that was complicated and expensive to overcome, due to planning regulations and conservation restrictions. I confess, sadly, that in each of these situations church ministry amongst older people did not feature on my radar. Ironically, for a number of those years I was working for a secular charity for older people, helping to establish community activities!

The COVID-19 pandemic forced churches to become less building-centric, and some of the creative innovations to promote togetherness that have emerged have the potential of lasting benefit. At the very least we have seen that there is still so much we can facilitate when we don't have the use of a building.

Partnering with other churches

As part of your planning process, you will hopefully be looking at what other churches in your area are doing amongst older people, as you don't want to duplicate. How about seeking to partner with another church? If they are hosting a monthly or fortnightly activity, perhaps your church could use their building on the weeks that their activity is not running. I absolutely love it when churches work together; I always imagine God looking upon it and smiling. I'm reminded of Psalm 133: 'How good and pleasant it is when God's people live together in unity... For there the LORD bestows his blessing, even life for evermore".[1] If there is not another local church already running an activity, you could plan something new together.

PARTNERING WITH A CARE HOME

In Chapter 5 we explored ways that churches can reach out to care home residents, none of which require a church building. There may be possibilities of taking initiatives a step further, such as running a coffee morning, or a singing group in a care home and inviting older people from the local community to join. From a care home's point of view this may be a good marketing opportunity, and it's great for local seniors to gain a positive view of care environments, rather than seeing them as dreaded places. Obviously, these ideas all need a good and trusting relationship with the care home management.

PARTNERING WITH A LOCAL CAFÉ, PUB OR RESTAURANT

It seems to be the most normal social thing these days to go out for coffee. How about partnering with a local coffee shop and creating a knit and natter group, or something similar? Negotiate a discount with the café for participants if you can, to encourage them along. Or hold a lunch group that meets in different local eateries. You will need to check the accessibility of the buildings and make sure the toilets are not up or down a flight of stairs, as so often is the case in restaurants.

Outdoor activities

People in the third age of life may enjoy outdoor exercise to keep fit and healthy, as well as socialising at the same time. Research shows that outdoor activity is good for our mental and physical wellbeing. This could be anything from a walking group, bowling, an outdoor gentle exercise class, or even walking football.[2] Recently, I heard of an allotment group for older people, where they not only get to socialise and do exercise, they also get to enjoy the satisfaction of growing edible produce.

Of course, outdoor activities are weather-dependent, so it's worth having a plan B, which could simply be meeting for refreshments at a local coffee shop, along with an effective means of communicating the change of plan at short notice.

Pastoral visiting and befriending schemes

Many churches have a team of trained pastoral visitors to call in on members of their church who are housebound or sick, so that they still feel a sense of belonging to their church community. There are also many isolated older people in our communities who would find it difficult to get to an activity at a church building but would value the company of a regular visitor. Rather than older people coming to you, consider training a group of volunteers to go to them. Linking Lives[3] is a Christian charity that works with churches and Christian agencies across the UK to set up befriending schemes, including a telephone befriending service that was developed during the pandemic. They provide the support and resources needed to start a project, including key operational documents and guidance at every stage of the journey. They estimate that it takes about six months to establish a new visiting project, from researching the need in your community and engaging with local agencies, to recruiting, training and placing volunteers.

LINKING LIVES FOREST OF DEAN

A church in the Forest of Dean was inspired by the Linking Lives model and believed it would make a difference in the lives of older people in the local area. Their heart is to be alongside those people who are hidden from view, knowing that as Christians they take Christ with them and share the hope, love and value that comes from Him.

This verse in Isaiah sums up their mission: 'He has sent [us] to comfort all those who are sad and to help the sorrowing people of Jerusalem [the Forest of Dean]. I will give them a crown to replace their ... sorrow, and clothes of praise to replace their spirit of sadness.'[4]

They started their Linking Lives scheme in 2016 and have seen those words from Isaiah brought to reality. One lonely older gentleman, who when referred to them lamented that he just wanted to 'go', now chuckles that he hopes he won't 'go' for a while! From small beginnings the project has grown so that they have befriended more than 50 people in their first three years and currently have 30 volunteers visiting 32 people.

There have been frustrations along the way, particularly the time it took to recruit volunteers even before the criminal record checks, references and training were carried out. They have had to learn to relax and to pray more, with the understanding that people can't be made to volunteer – it has to be in their hearts.

The second challenge was the time and planning it took to get other churches on board. Again letting go and understanding how churches operate has helped, knowing that it needs time, momentum, favour and trust to build those relationships, along with the knowledge that God goes before them. It is a journey, and it reflects what is done in befriending – being alongside, not rushing, being gentle and loving.

Along with the challenges there have been highlights,

particularly when hearing about the difference befrienders make in people's lives. One lady said, 'Thank you for giving me back my life!' They often come alongside people who have reached a low place, and to see the transformation in them is stunning and beautiful. When people journey from feeling unvalued and unloved to feeling esteemed and loved, after being introduced to someone to come alongside them as their friend, it is wonderful to behold! They have found that even the physical health of those befriended can improve, and friendship lifts depression, so that wellbeing and confidence rises.

The advice they would give to anyone considering starting a Linking Lives project is simply to go for it, knowing that it is a privilege and a joy.

Joy's story

Joy contacted the Linking Lives scheme in the Forest of Dean. This is her story, in her own words:

A while ago I was advised to contact Linking Lives by a social worker charged with social prescribing. At that time, I was poorly and had various chronic and degenerative conditions, and I was more than a little bit 'down'. I felt quite sorry for myself when I first called Emma, and totally embarrassed and inadequate to be asking for help. However, Emma sounded understanding and really enthusiastic on the phone, so it couldn't be too bad, could it? She arranged to visit after a few days, explained about Linking Lives, asked me quite a bit about myself and said it might take a while but 'be patient' because she wanted to find just the right person to be my befriender. (I didn't tell her that I seldom manage patience because it's just not built into my DNA.)

Emma was lovely, but I felt a bit of a failure for having to admit that I'm lonely and in need of a friend at all. Should be managing on my own – that sort of thing. After a few weeks, Emma returned together with Wendy. Since Wendy, my befriender entered my life, so much has changed.

We arranged to meet once a week and go out as often as possible. I use a wheelchair when outside the house but Wendy didn't seem at all deterred. She very willingly and easily popped the wheelchair in and out of the car and certainly didn't give the impression that pushing me around was a chore. (I was secretly listening for any sign of huffing and sighing in case it was getting too much effort.)

We had wonderful times together. We went *out* and for me to go *out* was a really rare and treasured treat. Smelling the earth; wind in my hair; feeling the sunshine; listening to and feeling part of the chatter and bustle in cafés. We went out lots; shopping and many cups of coffee and cake. We went to beauty spots, garden centres, Lydney Lake and park to see the ducklings, Gloucester Cathedral where we had an amazing day with Isabel and Pauline. Wendy and I became good friends. Knowing Wendy gave me so much – she, herself, was a gift.

She would come on a Monday, and it was as if the sun suddenly shone on my entire week, the remaining days being full of happy memories. We chatted a lot – about our families, religion, things that gave us joy.

Last autumn was a dark time. I experienced a lot of heartache with my daughters and Wendy was there. She was a rock. She gave up a lot of her time to helping me plough through the mud. She helped me emotionally and helped me to get things sorted out in a practical sense. She was there with her medical knowledge and reassurance when my youngest daughter had a quadruple bypass. I was a snivelling and drivelling wreck that day and don't think I would have managed to hold things together for my daughter or myself without Wendy's help. She has helped me to remain upright through difficult times. She's been there, just as you would want from a friend. Always kind and generous and giving of her time, her understanding, her acceptance and her love.

She also helped me to 'grow up'. I had a totally irrational lifelong fear of going to the doctor's. Of course GP's surgeries were second nature to Wendy. She took me often for appointments and gradually over time her confidence seemed to rub off on me. She always walked through life so 'lightly'. I no longer fear going, which shows that even after 70-odd years, there's still more 'growing up' to be done.

I suppose the area where Wendy touched my life most deeply was in my spirituality. When we first met I was a very sceptical agnostic/atheist who hadn't much time for God and religion and all that stuff. Wendy on the other hand was a profoundly religious person (whoever thought to put us two together? Emma?). In fact, I had never met anybody who lived and embodied her religious faith and principles in her daily life so strongly and beautifully as Wendy did. She was truly inspirational. But, the great thing was, she didn't push it. She knew where I stood and I knew where she stood, and each was respected.

But this thing, this 'religious thing' kept eating away at me. To see Wendy so committed, so devoted, so joyful and trusting. Living her beliefs in everything she did and always, always, wanting to help people – that was an eye-opener. To be honest, it was something I wanted – I wanted some of that but had no idea how it could possibly happen.

Then came the day when Wendy, Isabel, Pauline and I went to Gloucester Cathedral! Magical place! I thought we had gone on a tourists' day out to admire the architecture. Wrong! We went to a short midday communion service led by a lovely vicar called Mike (at least I think that was his name).

So here am I, an avowed agnostic (bordering on atheism), feeling very uncomfortable at a communion service. The stage is set – then wham! Something smacks me full in the chest and my world has changed forever. Well, this time it's not another heart attack! More like a love attack. It was a sense of utterly overwhelming love and power and glory, yet all wrapped in a sort of humility. Something so incredibly beautiful that it is way beyond my words to describe. An experience, some sort of deliciously, deeply other worldly experience that opened something up inside me that I didn't even know was there. Tears – many tears – but tears of love, of adoration, joy and of yearning, the yearning of the soul for union. Not what I had expected on a day trip to Gloucester.

So we went to the cathedral café for a pick-me-up coffee, though brandy might have been more appropriate. Wendy explained that the experience was like being touched by the Holy Spirit. I have no idea – still slightly sceptical, but I don't have a better understanding, so that's what I'm running with for now.

So, through Linking Lives and Wendy I have now made a connection with Christchurch in the Forest, and life has sort of gone off on a different track.

Emma recently asked me what I had gained through the Linking Lives befriending. I don't think she expected the answer of 'total transformation'. That's the important one. But there are many, many other gifts.

Friendships – I've met new people, been to new places and done new things, so I feel more hooked into life somehow – more engaged, and of course, not so lonely.

Because of the people I've met and the things I've done (lovely day at the Activity Centre; Xmas coffee morning at Emma's house, etc.) I feel more alive, more stimulated, so less bored (that interminable boredom when you're on your own and can't get out).

I've been blessed with loving, caring, practical support in the dark times when I've needed it most. I don't have to walk alone anymore.

Because the sun comes out on Monday, my week now has some structure to it. In fact, I actually know now which day of the week it is. When all the days are just a long, lonely, boring blur, it's very difficult to know a Tuesday from a Thursday. But now I have a social diary and I'm rather proud of that.

It's much easier too, when I'm not so well. It's rotten being poorly on your own when you haven't got the oomph to get up and make a cup of tea.

My lovely befriender would always pop in and keep an eye; have a chat and put the kettle on. I knew she was secretly checking up on me, but it was rather lovely to have someone around who would do that. Made me feel that I mattered.

So all in all, Linking Lives and its lovely volunteers have quite genuinely been a Godsend.

Joy has encountered and experienced something of the fullness of life that God desires for each of us, made possible through the work of Jesus. In the following chapter we'll explore more about mission and how we can point older people towards Jesus.

CHAPTER 8

MISSION

I have found this chapter the most challenging to write. Everything we do in reaching out in love to older people is mission, from lunch clubs, to befriending, to walking football. But what distinguishes us from the rest of the world, from secular organisations that offer lunch clubs, walking football and a myriad of other social activities? Are we in danger of becoming just another social opportunity? Don't get me wrong, social interactions are vital for our wellbeing, whatever our age, but if our mission amongst older people is limited to opportunities for socialising, that surely falls short of life in all its fullness. Our desire should be for older people to know the fullness of life God intends for them: His peace that passes understanding,[1] the joy unexplainable and hope for the future that comes from walking His path. I don't want to downplay the powerful witness of God's love – we have seen from the stories in this book the impact that can have on an individual's journey of faith. But I wonder whether there is also a place for being more intentional about giving older people the opportunity to explore Christian truths.

When I was in my teens and 20s I had a zeal for evangelism. I would happily be out on the streets talking to people about Jesus, or anywhere that the opportunity arose. I was clear about what the good news was, and how people needed to respond, and I witnessed people become Christians, receive miraculous healing and have their lives transformed. Fast forward 30 years and, if I'm honest, I can't remember the last time I shared the gospel with anyone. What has changed? Well, society has changed for starters: in our postmodern world few people want absolutes, and truth has become whatever you want it to be. It's viewed as arrogant and narrow-minded to declare that Jesus is 'the way and the truth and the life'.[2] When I trained and worked as a nurse, I had it drummed into me that I wasn't allowed to share my faith or pray with patients. So I guess I've changed as well; I've become timid about sharing my faith, more cautious about offending people, fearful of the repercussions and less willing to step out of my comfort zone. My thinking has become muddied too about what the gospel actually is, and what people need saving from. Is it just me? The gospel used to be so uncomplicated in my mind – there is a God who loves us, but sin has separated us from Him. Jesus opened the way through the cross for us to come back into relationship with God. Therefore, ABC: accept, believe, confess, or some other similar acronym. I would have tried to avoid any religious jargon in sharing the gospel and I might even have drawn a picture with two cliffs separated by a deep chasm, God on one side, us on the other, with the cross in the middle, connecting the two.

Perhaps it is still that simple, but it seems to be much more difficult (and potentially offensive) to share the gospel these days. Sin is an alien concept in our society and more associated with naughty treats when you're on a diet, than the condition of the human heart. It's much more comfortable to tell people that God loves them than to share the truths of the life, death and resurrection of Jesus. Of course, we want people to know that God loves them, but they also need to know part two of John 3:16: 'For God so loved the world *that he gave his one and only*

Son, that whoever believes in him shall not perish but have eternal life.'[3]

And so I'm challenged. I look at my own life: the peace that Jesus gives me in stormy situations, the forgiveness I receive on a regular basis, the joy I experience in knowing I am a much-loved daughter of the King, and the hope I have for the future. And I wonder why I'm not willing to take the risk of being rejected, or of having my reputation questioned so that others can know Jesus in a personal way and experience these things too.

When I was in my early 20s I went on a road trip around the western states of the USA with some friends. It was a whistle-stop tour of many incredible places including the Grand Canyon, which we saw briefly from one viewing point. I was disappointed. I had heard so much about the Grand Canyon, and yes, the view we saw was good, but it didn't leave me with the wonder and awe I was expecting. Many years later I returned to the Grand Canyon with my family, and we spent two days exploring, including getting up early to watch a sunrise. It was absolutely incredible – the majestic, mind-blowing beauty of creation.

What has this got to do with the gospel and our mission amongst older people? I fear that we (and I include myself in this) are in danger of reducing the gospel to one dimension that leaves people underwhelmed. People need the opportunity to explore the full panorama of truths presented in the good news, and to come into a life-transforming relationship with Jesus.

GOOD NEWS OR BAD?

One thing I have realised as I have been wrestling with this chapter is that I had lost sight of the fact that the gospel is *good* news. Subconsciously I have been viewing the gospel as *bad* news. The Bible does warn us that to some people the message of the cross is a 'stumbling-block ... foolishness',[4] or even 'an aroma that brings death'.[5] I guess for those people, the gospel does appear to be bad news, and perhaps they have the loudest voices in today's society and I have allowed myself to be influenced by them. But there is another, much more important side of the coin in these verses. The gospel is also 'an aroma that brings life',[6] 'the power of God and the wisdom of God'.[7]

Paul declares, 'I am not ashamed of the gospel, because it is the power of God that brings salvation to everyone who believes'.[8] Sadly, I have to admit that I had become ashamed and apologetic about the gospel. I have been looking at the gospel from the perspective of the world, and trying to make it more palatable to those who might find it difficult to swallow.

I make a mean chilli con carne, even if I do say so myself, and over the years it's become something of a trademark to those who have stepped over the threshold of my home. But there's been the odd occasion when I've omitted some of the seasoning, especially if I'm concerned that it might be too spicy for some of my guests, resulting in a less than satisfactory, bland version of the original. I think there are times too when I have served a one-dimensional, bland version of the gospel, to try to make it more palatable.

Let's be clear in our minds that the gospel is good news. Tom Wright, in his book *Simply Good News*,[9] reminds us that the early apostles thought the gospel was such good news that it was worth announcing as widely as possible. It's not just good advice that tells people how to live and what to do if they want to go to heaven, it's *news*. It's a declaration of something that has happened: that Jesus came to earth to show us what God was like, that He died and was resurrected, and through Him God has opened up the door to His new kingdom, which we are all invited into. It's not just a kingdom we go to after death, we experience it in the here and now, but in order to enter it we have to give up the way that we are going and walk a new path. Jesus is at the centre of the good news, who He is and the meaning of His life, death and resurrection.

I have been on a journey over the last few weeks, rediscovering the wonder of the gospel. Perhaps the first piece of good news for many people is simply the fact that there is a God, and more than that, He is a good God who loves them dearly. But that's only the beginning. There is more good news to come: this God who loves them and knows them intimately also wants them to know Him personally, not just know *about* Him. He has made that possible through the life, death and resurrection of Jesus. It doesn't stop there. He wants to empower people to live life in all its fullness through the Holy Spirit dwelling in them. And if all that wasn't enough good news, He wants to give them a hope for the future – that life in all its fullness continues beyond death, the grave is not the end!

How do people take hold of all that this good news is declaring? By believing it, giving up the path that they are walking and instead becoming an apprentice of Jesus, living life His way, with the help of the Holy Spirit.

THE GOSPEL OF THE CHURCH

We can also reduce the good news of Jesus to the gospel of the Church, when sharing the gospel simply becomes an invitation to church services. Just to clarify, there's nothing wrong with inviting people to church! But when that becomes a substitute for sharing the gospel we are again in danger of serving up a bland, one-dimensional gospel that leaves people underwhelmed. Because, let's face it (and please don't excommunicate me!), the Church isn't always a great reflection of the gospel. It's full of imperfect people who have the potential to make mistakes, hurt one another, and be hypocritical. People can have bad experiences of church and assume that is what God is like. It's not.

I love the Church, I love being part of a spiritual family and I would echo the advice of the writer of Hebrews, to 'not give up meeting together'.[10] The Church, operating at its best, points people towards Jesus in every aspect of its being. But there's no such thing as a perfect church this side of eternity.

Of course we want people to be welcomed into the church family and find a sense of belonging and community, but we also want them to come to a place of believing – believing in Jesus, not believing in the Church. The Church might let them down or fail to live up to their expectations, but Jesus will always be enough.

So, yes, let's demonstrate God's love through the activities we are offering, let's create opportunities to build relationships and let's invite people to church if that is appropriate. But let's also consider how we can communicate the good news of Jesus to those who are coming along. We need to give older people opportunities to explore these truths afresh. Perhaps they too have been underwhelmed by previous narrow glimpses of the gospel and the Church, or perhaps they have not heard, grasped and understood the good news. There is an urgency to reach the older generations as they are likely to have less time left to encounter the full wonder of the gospel.

Let's not allow ourselves to be influenced by the thinking of the world, but let's be transformed by the renewing of our minds[11] as we remind ourselves of the wonder and goodness of the gospel, so that we are convinced that it is good news worth announcing as widely as possible. Of course we need to do that sensitively, but let's do it! My prayer for myself is that I will be willing to step out of my comfort zone, risk my reputation and face my fear of rejection, so that older people have the opportunity to encounter Jesus. Jesus was willing to lay down His reputation, He was willing to be countercultural and do things that the influencers of His day looked down upon and criticised. We need the courage to follow in His footsteps.

GENERATIONAL WORLD VIEWS

How do we create opportunities for older people to explore the truths of the gospel? It's worth bearing in mind that each generation of older people may have been influenced by the prevailing world views of their era. Those born before 1945 will have been influenced by the Christian heritage of our nation. They are more likely to have attended Sunday school and learnt Bible stories as part of their education, so that they have a head knowledge of Christian stories, even if they don't understand the personal significance of them. Baby boomers, on the other hand, grew up in a generation that began to reject traditional Christianity, and was seeking other spiritual experiences. If you are particularly interested in reaching out to this younger generation of actively retired people, a short book has been written on *Reaching the Saga Generation*.[12] And there are new generations of actively retired people emerging all the time, who will have had unique life experiences and been influenced by different world views. As we look at tools that have been developed to enable older people to explore the claims of the Bible, we will need to consider which generation of older people they are most appropriate for.

ALPHA FOR SENIORS AND CHRISTIANITY EXPLORED

Alpha for Seniors is the regular Alpha course with large-print workbooks. Alpha is a tried and tested way of enabling people to explore the gospel and many have come to faith through it. The course may need to be adapted to suit your audience, bearing in mind that the most recent DVDs are geared up to a younger generation. Also, some older people find weekly sessions difficult to attend, due to other appointments and commitments, especially over ten weeks. Christianity Explored is a shorter course that has been used instead of Alpha for Seniors and found to work well. Some seniors' pastors have noted that facilitating discussion groups in the 'silent generation' (those born between 1925 and 1945) can be challenging, as they have been brought up 'to be seen and not heard', and initially may not be comfortable with being asked to express their opinions. This, of course, is a generational stereotype and not true for everyone born during those years, but it's worth bearing in mind if you are struggling to generate discussion in an Alpha or Christianity Explored group. When they are encouraged to feel that what they have to say is important, they often find their voice and are able to share freely. This comes from relationship and time spent getting to know one another.

Liz Stacey, from Winchester Baptist Church, slightly adapted Christianity Explored to meet the needs of her group. They met once a month, which seemed easier to commit to, and by the end of the five sessions all six participants made a prayer of commitment.

PILGRIM'S PROGRESS

During her years ministering to seniors, Liz Stacey noticed that many older people were afraid of dying, but no one would let them talk about it. She wanted to find a way of talking to them about life and death issues (without frightening them) and telling them the good news about Jesus and the wonderful future God had prepared for those who put their trust in Him. Using John Bunyan's *The Pilgrim's Progress*, she developed an interactive nine-session course, consisting of storytelling, drama, discussion and lots of fun. It is particularly aimed at older people who have no church background or personal faith, although it is relevant to everyone. The first group were in their 80s and 90s and over the weeks, as the participants journeyed with Christian (the main character in the story), their understanding of the Christian faith deepened, resulting in many of them making a personal commitment to the Lord.

The 'Pilgrim's Progress Interactive Study Guide' is now available to download for free.[13] An adaptation of *The Pilgrim's Progress* has been written by Geraldine McCaughrean[14] and is recommended for leaders to read alongside the study guide.

Many of the pre-baby boomer generation will be familiar with the story, having read adaptations of it at school. Interestingly, a new animation of *The Pilgrim's Progress* has been released, so it will be fascinating to see if it generates a revival of interest.

HYMNS WE LOVE

Pippa Cramer, who developed the successful Connections morning at Holy Trinity Claygate, realised that they needed to be more intentional about walking alongside guests in their journey of faith. They experimented with a number of courses and realised that using the term 'course' was actually off-putting to some older people, as it sounded educational, with the potential of a test at the end. Instead, they have developed a four-week *series* of Hymns We Love to share the gospel, which has proved popular. Each week uses a well-known hymn to reveal Bible truths, and includes a 15-minute talk. They have found that even people with dementia are able to participate as they remember the old hymns. 'How Great Thou Art'[15] explores the wonder of the creator God; 'Rock of Ages'[16] is an opportunity to talk about why Jesus had to die; 'Amazing Grace'[17] is the theme for week three and 'The Lord is My Shepherd'[18] in the final week unpacks the promise of God being alongside us when times are hard. At the end of the series, guests are invited to a special church service where all four hymns are sung, along with 'And Can it Be',[19] and the personal invitation of the good news is emphasised.

The series is available to listen to on the Daily Hope telephone line and as recordings on the Holy Trinity Claygate website.[20]

FAITH REDISCOVERED

Another course specifically designed for older people to explore the Christian heritage they grew up with is Faith Rediscovered, written by the minister of Hampton Wick Baptist Church, whose Crafty Cuppa group was mentioned in a previous chapter. It is a five-week course, available from CPO,[21] and each session lasts for about half an hour.

The purpose of all these tools is to provide an opportunity for older people to explore the wonderful truth of the good news and understand how it is relevant to their lives. Each tool should be used prayerfully, in an environment where older people feel loved and accepted, and safe to ask questions and share their thoughts. We are sowing seeds that God is able to water by the power of His Holy Spirit. Ecclesiastes encourages us: 'Keep on sowing your seed, for you never know which will grow – perhaps it all will.'[22]

CHAPTER 9

GETTING STARTED

Having explored numerous possibilities for growing a ministry amongst older people, you might well be feeling overwhelmed by choice and not know where to start, so in this chapter we'll look at some of the practical ways forward, whatever route you decide to take.

PRAYER

Unless the LORD builds the house, the builders labour in vain.'[1]

We can be full of good ideas and be excellent planners, motivators and organisers, but we need to start on bended knees, asking the Father what is on His heart for the older people in our church and in our wider community.

Recently I sensed God speaking to me about restoring the dignity and value of older people, as I was reading the story of Nehemiah rebuilding the walls of Jerusalem. I read of each household rebuilding the section of wall in front of their home and those with more resources rebuilding further. In a similar way, the dignity and worth of older people in our nation can be restored as each church rebuilds it within their community, and as each church plays its part in the restoration, the whole will be far greater than the individual parts.

But Nehemiah experienced opposition, and we should expect the same. The devil will oppose all that seeks to love and build up, for He comes to 'steal and kill and destroy'.[2] Nehemiah posted watchmen on the walls to enable the work to continue and I believe it's important that as we start new ventures to bring dignity, love and worth to older people that we also have watchmen alongside us, men and women who will pray faithfully, not just as the new work starts, but in an ongoing way.

So, I encourage you to invite a small team to pray regularly for the new ministry you are working towards. They may not be the people who will serve on your team, but they will be doing battle in the heavenlies. Share your ideas and thoughts with them as the vision of what is on God's heart for the older people in your area develops, and ask them to let you know anything they sense God might be saying as they pray.

You'll also need to submit your ideas humbly to your church leadership, as you want and need them to be supportive. It's worth sharing with them early in the journey so that they can be praying too, and together you can discover what is on God's heart.

DEVELOPING YOUR STRATEGY

I have to confess that I'm not always very good at being strategic – I'm a doer much more than a planner. I rush straight in, learn from my mistakes as I go along and by the grace of God, I've managed to muddle my way through. But in recent years, as I have run the charity Embracing Age, I've learnt that I need to be more strategic and that there is wisdom and effectiveness in taking time to think things through and plan. It's still not one of my strong points, but I'm learning, and it definitely helps for me to keep it simple.

There are three questions that I ask myself when I am trying to be strategic:

- Where are we now?
- Where do we want to be?
- How are we going to get there?

Within those three overarching questions are lots of other questions you can ask yourself to help get to your answers, but don't get bogged down in the minutiae – the idea is that the other questions help you answer those three big ones. Let's look at each question individually. Some of these questions might be difficult to answer but they are worth grappling with.

WHERE ARE WE NOW?

YOUR CHURCH

You want to get a snapshot of where your church is now when it comes to ministry amongst older people. Here are some of the questions you may want to ask:

1. What is the overall vision and mission of the church and where does ministry amongst seniors fit into this?
2. What is the percentage of older people in our congregation? Roughly what percentage of these are baby boomers/third age/fourth age?
3. How many older people in your congregation have a caring role? Do they feel supported and cared for?
4. What path of discipleship, if any, are we already journeying with older people, including any discipleship tools we are using?
5. How are we preparing people for retirement and enabling

them to discover God's purposes for this next season of their lives?

6. What activities are we already running for older people?
7. How accessible is our church building?
8. How are we journeying with people through their frailer years, so that they still feel loved and a part of our church community?
9. How are we supporting people with dementia?
10. What opportunities are we giving people to discuss death and dying?
11. How important is it to our church to reach out effectively to unchurched older people and enable them to explore the meaning of the life, death and resurrection of Jesus?
12. If it's helpful you could do a SWOT[3] analysis of where your church is at in your ministry amongst older people.

YOUR COMMUNITY

1. What is the percentage and age range of older people in our community? Your local council should have this information.
2. Where are the care homes and sheltered housing facilities for older people?
3. What activities/support services are already being run by other organisations and churches?
4. What support services are available for carers?
5. How are we currently reaching out to older people in our community?
6. Are there any specific needs or gaps in provision that we can identify in our local community?

WHERE DO WE WANT TO BE?

1. What do older people in our church say about how the church can come alongside, support and empower them?
2. What journey of discipleship do we want to travel with older people, starting from retirement?
3. Are there specific needs in our community that God is calling us to meet, to display His love in action? What are we going to do in response?

HOW ARE WE GOING TO GET THERE?

1. Are there activities we could run that would enable us to build relationships with unchurched older people?
2. What tools could we use to help disciple older people and enable unchurched older people to explore biblical truth?
3. Are there established models that could help us meet the needs of older people in our community?
4. Are there resources in our community that we can draw on – e.g. dementia training?
5. What examples of good practice are there in other places that we can learn from?
6. Are there other churches or organisations we could partner with?
7. What resources do we need?
8. What are our priorities in this area?
9. How will we evaluate the effectiveness of our work?

In a business strategising scenario your goals would be SMART: specific, measurable, achievable, realistic and timely, but the Church is not a business. If we set goals that are achievable and realistic we are not leaving much room for God to do more than we could 'ask or imagine'.[4] At the time of writing, I have a strategy day coming up in the next two weeks' time with the trustees of Embracing Age. As I have been reflecting on where we want to be and how we are going to get there I have been reminded of this prayer – commonly, though perhaps erroneously, attributed to Sir Francis Drake:

> Disturb us, Lord, when
> We are too well pleased with ourselves,
> When our dreams have come true
> Because we have dreamed too little,
> When we arrived safely
> Because we sailed too close to the shore.
>
> Disturb us, Lord, when
> With the abundance of things we possess
> We have lost our thirst
> For the waters of life;
> Having fallen in love with life,
> We have ceased to dream of eternity
> And in our efforts to build a new earth,
> We have allowed our vision
> Of the new heaven to dim.
>
> Disturb us, Lord, to dare more boldly,
> To venture on wider seas
> Where storms will show your mastery;
> Where losing sight of land,
> We shall find the stars.
> We ask you to push back
> The horizon of our hopes;
> And to push into the future
> In strength, courage, hope, and love.

As we strategise and plan, let's dare to be bold in our vision and thinking.

Recruit your team

As the vision unfolds, you will need a team to bring it into reality. Begin to ask the Lord to show you who you should ask. I remember when I started the charity Embracing Age, I needed three trustees and I just couldn't think who to ask. Eventually I decided to pray about it (why do we think of prayer as an afterthought sometimes?) and God immediately brought someone to mind who had not been on my radar. I invited him to be a trustee and after prayerful consideration, he accepted. If we are walking in the purposes of God, bringing to fruition His vision for older people in our community, we can be confident that He will provide all that we need!

Meet with your team regularly to pray together, develop the vision and discuss the practical outworkings of it. You want them to own it too.

Recruiting volunteers

As well as your core team, it may be that you need to recruit other volunteers to act as drivers, welcomers, servers, cake makers, food preparers, etc., depending on what activity you are planning. It can be helpful to write a short description for each of the roles you need filling, so that people know exactly what they are letting themselves in for. Advertise for your volunteers in the church news bulletins, by sharing the vision in the Sunday services and by asking individuals directly. People often respond more proactively to a personal invitation than to a general call for volunteers – you'll need to do both. Sometimes people need to hear the call a few times before they respond, and asking directly is often the most effective way.

Consider whether all your volunteers need to be Christians, or members of your church. My experience has been that church members are often busy with so many responsibilities that it can be challenging to introduce a new opportunity to serve. But there may be people in your local community with a heart for older people who would love to serve at a lunch club, or as a driver or befriender, etc. At Embracing Age, we have many volunteers who are not churchgoers, but I am convinced that you don't need to be a Christian to play a game of chess with a care home resident or accompany them on a walk! You can build new links between your church and the community by recruiting volunteers from outside your four walls.

Many places will have a Volunteering Centre where you can advertise for volunteers, as well as community noticeboards and a myriad of social media opportunities like Twitter, Facebook and community websites. Of course, when you are recruiting new volunteers, whether those outside or within the church, you will need stringent vetting procedures and safeguarding practices.

Think about the qualities and skills you are looking for in volunteers and bear in mind that some skills can be taught, such as how to serve food, but some qualities, such as friendliness and patience, are not so easily instilled. You may not need friendliness and patience to help with the washing up, but you will certainly need them to befriend an older person, or host a lunch club table. If you have concerns about the suitability of a volunteer who has applied for a role it is acceptable to turn them down, or perhaps offer them a different role that is more supervised.

SAFEGUARDING

Churches should already have safeguarding policies and procedures, but it's worth checking they are up to date, include working with adults at risk, and cover the roles your volunteers will be undertaking, such as befriending.

Discuss the activity you are pioneering with the nominated safeguarding officer at your church so that you are clear about the procedures for recruiting new volunteers. Not all volunteer activities will qualify to have a criminal record check, so you will need to discuss the different roles volunteers will be undertaking with the safeguarding officer, or the organisation you use to process the checks,[5] who should be able to advise. All volunteers should provide details for you to take up two references, and also complete a self-disclosure form. If you are recruiting drivers, you should see a copy of their driver's licence and up to date car insurance.

POLICIES, PROCEDURES AND INSURANCE

Depending on the activity you are starting, you will need to ensure that other policies and procedures are in place, such as confidentiality, or lone visiting, if volunteers will be seeing older people in their homes. Also that risk assessments have been undertaken. This is an area where working with an established model can be helpful as they will have thought all these aspects through and have policies and procedures that you can adopt, and will be able to support you through these processes.

You will also need to check that your church insurance covers the activities that your volunteers will be undertaking.

VOLUNTEER TRAINING

Consider the different roles the volunteers will be undertaking and whether they will need training. Those preparing meals will need food hygiene training; welcomers may need some training as to how to make people feel at ease; volunteers at a memory café will need dementia training; befrienders will need training in lone visiting, listening, boundaries, safeguarding, etc. If you are working with established models, they may be able to provide the training for you, otherwise you will need to source it elsewhere. Some training, such as safeguarding and food hygiene, may be available online.

Marketing and advertising

If your activity or project is going to be successful, people need to know about it! Ask yourself the following questions:

1. Who are the people we are trying to reach out to with this activity? Is it the actively retired, people in the fourth age of life, retired men, people living with dementia and their loved ones, carers, etc.?
2. Where are these people? In the fourth age of life they may be in sheltered accommodation or care homes, or they may be housebound.
3. How will you reach them? If you have a parish magazine that is delivered to every home in your area, you have a great means of communication (although, of course, there's no guarantee that people read it!). You could put posters on community noticeboards (many supermarkets have these) or fliers in libraries. Word of mouth is also very effective, encouraging older people in your church to invite their friends.
4. Are there other organisations who could spread the word for you? For example, if you are reaching out to people with dementia, you could find out if there are organisations that support carers who could put something in their newsletter. Or, if you are seeking to reach out to people who are housebound, you could see if there are care agencies who would spread the word for you. If you are reaching actively

retired people, then you could try your local U3A (University of the Third Age).

5. What communication do you need to produce? For example: fliers, posters, webpages, tweets, promotional videos, etc. Make sure these are done with excellence, as this is the first impression people will get about your church and the activity you are facilitating.

If only a few people turn up during your first few weeks, don't be disheartened. Continue to look for new channels to spread the word. Of course, if people are not coming back after the first visit or two, you may need to ask yourself why and seek out some honest feedback.

SUPPORTING VOLUNTEERS

It's so easy to take people for granted, especially in a church setting where members are willing to serve sacrificially. The reality is that we all like to feel appreciated sometimes and to feel that our input is making a difference. Remember to thank your volunteers regularly and ensure that they feel supported in their roles. If you have a large team of volunteers, delegate this to some of your core team – give them each specific volunteers to support, and let your focus be supporting your core team. Volunteers who are lone working, such as befrienders, may need extra support and will need to know who to contact if they experience problems or have concerns while they are out visiting.

General appreciation and support can be shown through regular volunteer gatherings, whether termly, bi-annually or yearly; sending occasional thank you cards; pairing new volunteers with more experienced ones in a buddy system; and passing on any feedback you receive about the difference they are making.

LAUNCHING

Set a launch date well in advance as it's always good to have a deadline to be working towards. Be realistic about it, discuss it with the church leadership and with your team. You may want to run a pilot session with just a few guests before your official launch as a practise run, depending on what activity you decide to facilitate. Give yourself plenty of time to allow for recruiting and training any other volunteers you need, and advertising the activity widely.

It's good to discuss with your church leaders the idea of commissioning the team during a Sunday service close to the launch date. In this way the church can pray for you all, and the team will have a strong sense that the church is supportive and totally behind this new ministry.

Before the launch, set a date in three to six months' time to review the first few months – what's gone well; what have you learned; what could be improved upon? Of course, you'll be on a steep learning curve from the outset and you don't have to wait three to six months to make any necessary changes, but it can be helpful and encouraging to have a formal review with your team, and if you don't put a date in the diary it's the sort of thing that might just slip.

MEASURING AND COMMUNICATING YOUR IMPACT

What does success look like? When you review your project or activity after the first six months, what criteria will you use to judge its effectiveness? The number of people who come along? The difference you have made in people's lives? But what difference are you seeking to make and how will you know if you have made that difference? Does success even matter if we are being faithful to what we believe God has called us to do?

These are interesting questions to consider before you start your new initiative. Those of us working in the charity sector, who are required to report back to funders, are acutely aware of the need to measure outcomes. We are accountable to the organisations and people who have invested in our work, and they want to know the difference their investment has made. The requirement to report back to funders may not be a necessity in a church-backed venture, but the principles of accountability, transparency and evaluation are still good practice. Here are some good reasons to measure your impact:

1. You can see how your project has grown (or not) over time.
2. You will learn about the impact your project has made in the lives of participants, which is hugely encouraging for everyone involved.
3. You can evaluate what isn't working and make necessary changes so that you are developing and improving.
4. You can be confident in the aspects that are working well.
5. You can communicate the difference you are making to the wider Church and others, and generate more interest.
6. You have evidence of the difference you are making if you are ever looking for external funding.
7. Inviting feedback keeps us humble and willing to take on board constructive criticism.

Here are some tips on how to evaluate your work:

1. Keep it simple. You don't want to generate loads of data that takes ages to analyse.
2. Be clear about what you want to know. Perhaps it is just the number of people attending your activity. Make sure you have an easy way to collect and store this information. This is

helpful information, but it doesn't tell you anything about the difference you are making in people's lives.

3. Collect stories. Numerical data has some use, but nothing is more powerful than the stories of lives impacted, as you hopefully will have experienced as you read the accounts of various individuals in this book.

4. Invite feedback from participants.

5. Use simple, validated tools only if appropriate to your situation, such as a loneliness scale[6] or wellbeing questionnaire.[7]

6. Keep your evaluation proportionate to the size of your project. If you are embarking on a large venture with outside funding, then your monitoring and evaluation procedures will need to be detailed and stringent. If you are running an activity with a small group, then your evaluation may be far more informal. But in either case, feedback is still vital and helpful to ensure that you are meeting the needs you set out to meet. It is also hugely encouraging to your team of volunteers to hear about the impact of the time and energy they are giving.

Case study: evaluating Embracing Age

The goal of Embracing Age is to reduce the loneliness experienced by care home residents and improve their quality of life. There are a whole host of loneliness and wellbeing scales that could be used to measure these things, but we have some serious challenges when working with some of the oldest and frailest people in society, not least that they are on a downward trajectory. The care home is likely to be their last earthly dwelling, with the average length of stay between one and three years before death, depending on whether it's a residential home or a nursing home. You can't really do simple before and after measurements and expect to see an improvement!

Secondly, an estimated 80 per cent of care home residents have some degree of dementia or significant memory loss, and their feelings of wellbeing can change from day to day, or hour to hour, due to a multitude of factors. And it's a degenerative disease – it's only going to get worse. Again, challenging to measure impact over time.

But we still want to know whether we are making a difference in people's lives, so as a small organisation with limited resources we have devised a straightforward and simple way to monitor our effectiveness:

1. We measure the time volunteers spend with residents: this is a simple numerical value we can easily gather. Furthermore, when working with people with dementia the most important thing is that they enjoy the 'in the moment' experience, because they are living in the moment. Measuring quality time spent with residents is part of the way we do that, by volunteers logging their time online, using a google form. But how do we know it is *quality* time? This is our second measurement tool. We send an annual survey to our volunteers using another Google form. We are looking to see that residents have enjoyed the 'in the moment' experience of time spent with volunteers – so we ask volunteers things like:

- What do you do with residents?
- What signs do the residents you visit show of enjoying the time that you spend with them? (This may seem obvious, but some residents struggle with verbal communication, so a sign may be something non-verbal, such as a smile, laughter, or a squeeze of the hand.)
- Please tell us any stories or anecdotes about your volunteering experience.

2. We want to hear more than just the views of volunteers, so we send a short survey to care home managers – they are generally very busy so we just ask two quick questions:

- Would they recommend our service to other care home managers?
- Do our volunteers improve the quality of life of the residents they visit?

3. Last, but by no means least, we interview two residents who have capacity and ask them about the difference having a volunteer has made to their lives. This provides us with lovely stories and quotes, as well as potential constructive criticism.

Often I will sit at my computer and cry when I read the stories that volunteers and residents share with us, stories that we would not have heard if we had not asked. In the end, that is why we are involved in ministry amongst older people, because we want to make a difference, we want to be ministers of God's love, compassion and hope. We want older people, whether in the third or fourth age of life, to know that they are valued, appreciated and deeply loved. We want them to experience later life in all its fullness.

SUSTAINABILITY

You will want to develop a ministry that is sustainable. One of the strengths of the Church is that it is historically rooted in local communities and is there for the long haul – it has been around for 2,000 years! Whilst you might not be expecting your ministry amongst seniors to continue to the next millennium, you will still want to ensure that it has longevity. Three common reasons for a venture to flounder are lack of manpower, lack of finances or dwindling numbers of participants.

MANPOWER

If you are supporting your team of volunteers in the ways outlined earlier in this chapter, and if you are inspiring enthusiasm through regularly feeding back stories about the difference they are making, you are likely to hold on to your team for longer. But even so, the reality is that people move, become ill and have changes in their life circumstances, which mean they need to stop volunteering. Always be on the lookout for new team members, and share regularly with the church about the impact you are making so that it is something people are keen to be involved with. Don't wait until you're desperate!

Also keep an eye open for people you can raise up as leaders. Don't make yourself indispensable – it only creates stress and pressure for you, and can result in burnout if you end up taking on too much. There is something quite liberating about appreciating how dispensable we are! Besides which, we are all getting older and you will not be able to be at the helm forever.

You may recall the story of St Stephen's Monday lunch club which was led by the couple who pioneered it until they were well into their 90s. When they retired there was no one in the congregation to take over the lead. Rather than closing it down, the seniors' pastor took on the responsibility, but ideally this shouldn't have been her role. We need to be on the lookout for future leaders and allow them to lead with us, gradually delegating responsibility to them. You want to feel confident that if you were absent for whatever reason, the show will go on as excellently as ever without you. We will talk more at the end of this chapter about the heart and mindset of a leader, so that they give from the overflow of all that God is pouring into their lives.

FINANCES

We discussed in an earlier chapter whether to charge a small amount for the activity you are running. Ideally you want to cover your costs so that you are financially sustainable. However, this is not always appropriate, especially if you are offering befriending services or similar. Charitable grants may be available for some activities, but these are usually for a fixed time period, so you may still need to consider other forms of fundraising. For small projects, this could be as simple as a coffee morning; for larger projects, you will need to be more creative. Ideally you want your income to be sourced from various streams, so that if one stream runs out you are not left high and dry. There are lots of online training and resources about fundraising available at low cost or free to small charitable organisations that you may be eligible to tap into.[8]

DWINDLING NUMBERS

There is a season for everything,[9] Solomon wisely instructs us. If numbers are dwindling, it might be time to be prayerfully sensitive to the changing of a season. An activity that was popular with a group of seniors during a certain era may no longer be attractive to the next generation of seniors.

However, numbers may dwindle for reasons that have nothing to do with the changing of a season. It could simply be that your publicity needs updating and your marketing needs a new strategy. Before decisions are made, it is wise to collect and prayerfully reflect on constructive feedback from participants and volunteers. As you do this with the rest of your team, your prayer supporters and the leadership of your church, you will gather a sense of whether the season is changing, and something new is needed, or whether you just need to tweak aspects of what you are currently doing.

LEADING FROM THE OVERFLOW

We have considered God's heart towards older people, the many activities that can be established in ministering amongst seniors, and the practicalities involved. At the close of this book we turn inward, to look at ourselves as leaders. John Maxwell tells us that everything rises and falls on leadership, and that is quite a responsibility. Often ministry amongst older people does not take centre stage in the life of the church, and leading on the sidelines can be a lonely place. That's one of the reasons it's so important to have the backing of your church leadership, a team approach and prayer support. Isolation saps our energy, crushes our vision and leaves us vulnerable to attack from the enemy.

Healthy leadership takes us back to the principles at the start of this book about what it means to be human. Our value and our worth come from who we are in Christ, not from anything we do or don't do, or any position of authority we hold. Our primary calling in life is as a son or daughter of the King of kings: 'to glorify God, and to enjoy him forever'.[10] Our ministry amongst seniors, as important as it is, remains secondary. This is easy to acknowledge in theory, but the reality can be quite different. I remember a time when although I still sensed passionately God's heart for the frail elderly, I felt constantly drained and exhausted, and experienced no joy in my work. I was perturbed by this and asked God about it, and have never forgotten the revelation He gave me. He showed me that I had put ministry first, so that subtly and gradually it had taken primary place. It can be so easy to do; after all, ministry amongst older people is an important and noble cause. Rather than partnering with God in what He was doing, I was taking all the responsibility on myself, and it was stealing my joy. In Matthew 11:30, Jesus says His 'yoke is easy' and His 'burden is light' – we are not meant to carry the weight by ourselves. I was doing God's work, but not in His way, and I needed to realign myself.

Here are some of the ways this happened for me.

ROLES AND RESPONSIBILITIES

God gave me a fresh revelation of my identity in Him, that before anything else I am His much-loved daughter. Nothing I do adds or takes away from that. I can rest secure in who I am in Him. I walk as a daughter of the King by seeking to love Him with all my heart, soul, mind and strength; to love others as He loves; to forgive others as He forgives; to show others what God is like and let my life point to Him. If I do nothing else, that will be enough. I should add that I'm not very good at walking as a daughter like this! But the point is that God loves me anyway – I don't strive to do these things to earn His love; He loves me with all my failings. I long to walk like this because I love Him, not to earn His approval.

God also showed me that He is the senior partner in the work that we do – in taking on all the responsibility myself I had lost His perspective. He actually cares about older people more than I do, and can manage quite well without me. But He gives me the privilege of partnering with Him in His work. All I need to do is be faithful and committed to the tasks He gives me – success or failure is in His hands.

When our identity is firmly rooted in Christ, we can hold our roles lightly in open hands, ready to be led by Him and willing to lay our roles down if He calls us to. We can also raise up others and release them to go beyond where we have reached and be joyful in their success, since it is all for His kingdom and His glory.

Rest and recreation

This was one of the areas I was not doing God's work in God's way. Even God rested, and yet I failed to carve out Sabbath time. Much of the work I do involves being with volunteers, and weekends are often a time when they are free, so I would book in meetings and training sessions on Sundays. Then I would wonder why my energy and joy were sapped. I have learnt the hard way that rest is important. We need to recharge our batteries; we can't give from the overflow if we are running on empty. I am now intentional about keeping a Sabbath day, and usually for me this is a Sunday, but it doesn't have to be. The point is to have a day when you switch off from work, when you choose not to read your emails and instead do activities that help you relax and unwind. I love to do creative stuff, like craft or knitting and crochet, or curl up with a good book. I'm also quite partial to binge-watching a TV series, but I'm not entirely sure how restful that actually is!

It's also important for your wellbeing to have regular recreation. For me this is going for a walk, cycling or kayaking. These are things that I love to do that also provide physical exercise and get me outdoors. What are the things you love to do? Give yourself permission and time to pursue them.

Reading and reflection

Along with rest and recreation, God is helping me to build other sustainable practices in to my life that enable me to receive from Him and give out from the overflow. I'll let you into a secret. One of my favourite things to do in the morning, after I have done the things I need to as a mum (make lunch for my youngest daughter and see her off to school) is to make a cup of tea, sit in bed and read the Bible and pray. I spent years feeling like this was a guilty pleasure, until I realised that for me it is a fundamental sustainable practice. It is where I am nourished and refreshed.

I have come to realise that reading the Bible regularly in this way feeds my Spirit. It is not that I have incredible revelation from God's word on a daily basis, or that I am diligent about asking all the right questions to apply it to my life. I just read, and somehow this feeds spiritual nutrients to my soul, just as the routine of eating healthy food nourishes our bodies without us really being aware of it. In fact, the time I am most aware of the good it does me is when I stop reading the word regularly and then feel spiritually depleted.

There's a danger that I'll come across as a super-disciplined saint here, which my family would happily and strongly refute! The reality is that I am not very good at engaging regularly in these sustainable practices, although I am becoming aware more quickly when I am in danger of running on empty, so at least that's a start. The idea is not that we walk under a cloud of condemnation for not doing the things we know are good for us. But we can work towards understanding the practices that will be sustaining for each of us individually and try to embed them into our lives on a more regular basis, in the gracious knowledge we need do nothing to win God's approval. We are loved!

That is where our ministry amongst older people starts and finishes, understanding how much older people are loved and valued by the creator of the universe, and knowing that we too are deeply loved.

Notes

Chapter 1: A Great Place to Grow Old

[1] Office for National Statistics, Estimates of the very old, including centenarians (ONS, 2018).

[2] Office for National Statistics, National population projections: 2016-based (ONS, 2017).

[3] Office for National Statistics, Living Longer: How our population is changing and why it matters, (ONS, 2018).

[4] NCVO, UK Civil Society Almanac, 2018.

[5] Age UK, Later Life in the United Kingdom (Age UK, 2018).

[6] Peter Brierley, The Ageing Church (Tonbridge, Brierley Consultancy, 2015).

[7] A theory developed by Peter Laslett in the 1980s.

[8] For a more in-depth read I recommend John Swinton's book Dementia, Living in the Memories of God (Grand Rapids, MI, William B. Eerdmans, 2012) on which these thoughts are based.

[9] John Stott, The Radical Disciple (Nottingham: IVP, 2010), pp.112-113

[10] Luke 9:3.

[11] Gen. 1:27

[12] Gen. 2:7

[13] Matt. 25:40, The Message.

[14]   I John 3:1.

[15]   Rom. 5:8.

[16]   John 3:16.

[17]   Rom. 8:38–39.

[18]   Gen. 2:18.

[19]   J. Holt-Lunstad, T. B. Smith, and J. B. Layton, Social relationships and mortality risk: a meta-analytic review (PLoS medicine, vol. 7, no. 7, 2010).

[20]   Age UK, Loneliness Evidence Review: Loneliness in Later Life (Age UK, 2015).

CHAPTER 2: LOOK, LISTEN, LOVE

[1]   www.housingcare.org

[2]   www.afterworknet.com

[3]   Prov. 15:22.

[4]   I Cor. 13:4–8.

[5]   John 13:35.

[6]   John 10:10 NCV.

[7]   Ps. 29:11.

[8]   John 16:33.

[9]   Gal. 5:22.

[10]   Isa. 46:4.

[11]   Isa. 26:3.

[12]   Emphasis mine.

[13]   John 15:4

[14]   Phil. 4:7.

[15]   I Tim. 6:17.

[16]   Billy Graham, Nearing Home (Nashville, TN, Thomas Nelson, 2011), p.91.

CHAPTER 3: DEMENTIA

1 https://www.alzheimers.org.uk/about-us/news-and-media/facts-media

2 www.liftedcare.com/metaphors-analogies-and-the-lived-experience-of-dementia

3 Dr Gemma Jones, *Care-Giving in Dementia, Volume 3: Research and Applications* (Brunner-Routledge, 2004), pp.46–63.

4 Dr Jennifer Bute with Louise Morse, *Dementia from the Inside* (London, SPCK, 2018).

5 Tom Kitwood, Dementia Reconsidered (Philadelphia, PA, Open University Press, 1997), p.82.

6 Bute, with Morse, *Dementia from the Inside.*

7 Col. 3:12,14.

8 https://youtu.be/CrZXz10FcVM

9 https://youtu.be/OfZxM6jTr9s

10 https://youtu.be/fyZQf0p73QM

11 Steven Morris, *Memory Café: How to Engage with Memory Loss and Build Community*, (Cambridge, Grove Books Ltd., 2017).

12 https://lyricsandlunch.org/start-a-group/

CHAPTER 4: CARERS

1 Gal. 6:2.

2 Edmond Budry (1854–1932). Translated into English by Richard Birch Hoyle (1875–1939).

3 Albert Jewell et al., The faith of primary carers of persons with dementia (*Journal of Religion, Spirituality and Ageing*, 28:4, 2016), pp.313–337.

4 http://www.carersconnected.uk

5 https://www.dementiapathfinders.org

6 Ron and Michael's stories are reproduced with kind permission from the Diocese of Liverpool, where they featured in

an article on their website, and with the blessing of Ron and Michael.

CHAPTER 5: CARE HOMES

1 Christina Victor, *Loneliness in care homes: a neglected area of research?* (Aging Health, 8:6, 2012), pp.637–646.
2 You can view her painting here: https://www.embracingage. org.uk/news/jeans-story
3 Heb. 13:5.
4 Isa. 46:4.
5 https://www.embracingage.org.uk/servicesincarehomes.html
6 http://www.parche.org.uk
7 https://www.storiesforthesoul.org/
8 https://www. embracingage.org.uk/servicesincarehomes.html
9 https://www.annachaplaincy.org.uk
10 https://www.annachaplaincy.org.uk
11 https://www.embracingage.org.uk/intergenerational
12 https://www.truthbetold.org.uk

CHAPTER 6: ACTIVITIES IN CHURCH BUILDINGS

1 https://www.churchofengland.org/more/church-resourc-es/churchcare/advice-and-guidance-church-buildings/accessibility; https://www.throughtheroof.org/forchurch-es/churchresources/; https://www.livability.org.uk/blog/community-engagement-blog/love-surpassing-knowl-edge-more-than-ramps-understanding-and-implementing-ac-cessibility/
2 https://www.sightlossfriendlychurch.org.uk
3 https://www.dementiafriends.org.uk/
4 https://www.dementiafriendlychurch.org.uk/

5   https://www.livability.org.uk

6   2 Tim. 3:16.

7   Freely available at https://embracingage.org.uk/ministryamongstseniors

8   Age to Age. Available from olderpeoplesministries@salvationarmy.org.uk

9   https://www.embracingage.org.uk/ministryamongstseniors

Chapter 7: No Building, No Problem

1   Ps. 133:1,3.

2   https://thewfa.co.uk

3   https://linkinglives.uk/

4   Isa. 61:3 NCV.

Chapter 8: Mission

1   Phil. 4:7.

2   John 14:6.

3   Emphasis mine.

4   1 Cor. 1:23.

5   2 Cor. 2:16.

6   2 Cor. 2:16.

7   1 Cor. 1:24.

8   Rom. 1:16.

9   Tom Wright, *Simply Good News* (London, SPCK, 2015).

10   Heb. 10:25.

11   Rom. 12:2

12   Chris Harrington, Reaching the Saga Generation (Cambridge, Grove Books, 2008)

13   www.embracingage.org.uk/pilgrims-progress

14   Geraldine McCaughrean, *A Pilgrim's Progress* (London, Hodder Children's Books, 2001).

15 Carl Boberg (1859–1940). Translated into English by Stuart Hine (1899–1989).

16 Augustus Toplady (1740–78).

17 *John Newton* (1725–1807).

18 'The Lord's My Shepherd', Francis Rous (c. 1581–1659).

19 Charles Wesley (1707–88).

20 https://www.htclaygate.org/; Pippa Cramer, pastoral care and seniors minister, pippacramer@htclaygate.org

21 https://www.cpo.org.uk/

22 Eccles. 11:6 The Living Bible.

CHAPTER 9: GETTING STARTED

1   Ps. 127:1.

2   John 10:10.

3   Strengths, weakness, opportunities, threats.

4   Eph. 3:20.

5   For example, https://thirtyoneeight.org

6   For more information on measuring loneliness read this article from the ONS: https://www.ons.gov.uk/peoplepopula-tionandcommunity/wellbeing/methodologies/measuringlone-linessguidanceforuseofthenationalindicatorsonsurveys

7   E.g. Warwick Edinburgh scale: https://warwick.ac.uk/fac/sci/med/research/platform/wemwbs/

8   E.g. Small Charities Coalition https://www.smallcharities.org.uk/ or the FSI www.thefsi.org

9   Eccles. 3:1.

10 Westminster Shorter Catechism.